VALUE PRESUPPOSITIONS IN THEORIES OF HUMAN DEVELOPMENT

Edited by

Leonard Cirillo
Seymour Wapner
Clark University

LEA LAWRENCE ERLBAUM ASSOCIATES, PUBLISHERS

1986   Hillsdale, New Jersey   London

Copyright © 1986 by Lawrence Erlbaum Associates, Inc.
  All rights reserved. No part of this book may be reproduced in
  any form, by photostat, microform, retrieval system, or any other
  means, without the prior written permission of the publisher.

Lawrence Erlbaum Associates, Inc., Publishers
365 Broadway
Hillsdale, New Jersey 07642

Library of Congress Cataloging-in-Publication Data
Main entry under title:

Value presuppositions in theories of human development.

  Derived from a conference sponsored by the Heinz
Werner Institute, Clark University, and held June 10–11,
1983.
  Includes bibliographies and indexes.
  1. Developmental psychology—Philosophy—Congresses.
2. Values—Psychological aspects—Congresses. 3. Moral
development—Congresses. I. Cirillo, Leonard.
II. Wapner, Seymour, 1917–   . III. Heinz Werner
Institute of Developmental Psychology. [DNLM: 1. Human
Development—congresses. 2. Psychology, Social—
congresses. 3. Social Values—congresses.
BF 778 V2145 1983]
BF712.5.V35 1986   155   85–16235
ISBN 0–89859–753–6
Printed in the United States of America
10 9 8 7 6 5 4 3 2 1

Contents

List of Contributors

RICHARD J. BERNSTEIN
Department of Philosophy
Haverford College, Haverford, Pennsylvania

JEROME S. BRUNER
Department of Psychology
New School for Social Research, New York, New York

CAROL GILLIGAN
Center for Moral Education
Harvard University, Cambridge, Massachusetts

JEROME KAGAN
Department of Psychology and Social Relations
Harvard University, Cambridge, Massachusetts

BERNARD KAPLAN
Department of Psychology
Clark University, Worcester, Massachusetts

MARX W. WARTOFSKY
Department of Philosophy
Bernard Baruch College, New York, New York

Preface

The chapters and discussions presented in this volume derive from the conference, Value presuppositions in theories of human development, sponsored by the Heinz Werner Institute, Clark University, on June 10–11, 1983. The conference included both psychologists and philosophers and mainly concerned those assumptions about what ought to be that enter into the ways that investigators in the human sciences construe development. The selection of these participants and this topic expresses one of the aims of the Heinz Werner Institute: to foster collaborative inquiry by members of different disciplines who are interested in the promotion of human development. Choosing this topic at this particular time reflects two important concerns: the implications for developmental psychology of the ongoing debate over foundations in many disciplines, from philosophy of science to literary criticism, and the current dangers of restricting developmental theory to cognition and epistemology narrowly conceived.

We wish to thank our fellow members of the Executive Council of the Heinz Werner Institute for help in planning the conference: Sybil S. Barten, Sandor Brent, Margery B. Franklin, Joseph Glick, Bernard Kaplan, Jonas Langer, Angel M. Pacheco, Roy Pea, and George Rand. Margery B. Franklin, Sarah Lawrence College, is also due our gratitude for taking on the responsibility of moderating the general discussion. We express our appreciation as well to Arthur Rummel and other members of the Clark University community who helped in organizing the proceedings. Finally, we are immensely grateful to Maryjane Minor for her outstanding work in the preparation of the conference and of this volume.

Leonard Cirillo
Seymour Wapner

Introduction

Although the development of values, especially moral values, is a lively subject of investigation in psychology and related disciplines, the theories and methods involved in this investigation are themselves often treated as independent of value considerations. The segregation of responsible inquiry from value judgments has been an explicit issue of debate in sociology since Max Weber's writings early in this century (Weber, 1949) but has played a more peripheral role in psychology. The major argument offered in favor of value-free inquiry is that freedom from bias is a precondition for truth as opposed to mere opinion (Kaplan, 1964). The pursuit of objective knowledge demands the suspension of value judgments. This position, as Weber himself emphasized, is itself a value judgment and appeals to values thought to constitute scientific work—unbiased observation, dispassionate analysis, valid reasoning, and so forth. MacIntyre (1978) has referred to the scientific community as ''one among the moral communities of mankind,'' noting that, ''objectivity is a moral concept before it is a methodological concept, and the activities of natural science turn out to be a species of moral activity'' (p. 37).

With respect to theories of development, we pose two kinds of value questions. One kind of question concerns normative facts: What values are espoused by developmental theorists? What values are ingredient in their work? What is the relationship between their espoused values and their values in action? The second kind of question concerns our own value judgments about these norms: What values *should* we espouse? What values *ought* to regulate our inquiry? What values *should* a theory of human development embody?

In the chapters and discussions to follow, the contributors confront these and connected questions directly, considering not only those values that they study in others but their own as well insofar as these shape the questions they pose, the methods of answering them, and the meanings ascribed to findings. Usually, because the phenomena we are studying occupy the foreground, the values from which our work proceeds fade into the background. Here, we attempt a figure-ground reversal: The usual objects of study recede from view as the contributors face squarely the value presuppositions of developmental theories.

To help guide the reader, we briefly summarize each of the chapters to follow, saving for the concluding chapter some comments on the issues raised by these chapters and by the critical discussions.

Richard Bernstein locates the theme of the conference as a part of our contemporary anxiety that there are no stable foundations to be found in any discipline and, further, that our most probable telos is self-annihilation. He shows how presuppositions about moral values fundamental to Western thought have been persistently called into question, ending with Nietschean skepticism about the very concept of moral and social development. These considerations appear to have led us toward radical relativism and toward abandoning any pretensions to a general theory of human development. But among those currently contributing in different, sometimes opposed, ways to this critique, Bernstein detects the emergence of a common vision: the need to foster "the telos of dialogical communities" in which experiences of solidarity and mutual understanding will keep alive the idea of moral and social development.

Jerome Bruner, in agreement with Bernstein's reminder that "pluralism is not radical relativism," maintains that developmental theories prescribe, not merely describe, "alternative optimal ways of achieving certain outcomes." Because the value positions taken in doing this cannot be read off from the facts, developmental theory is impossible without a base of valuational axioms. Unless we examine these value presuppositions, developmental theory takes the risk of canonizing beliefs implicit in the culture as though they were "natural," right, and without alternative. A case in point, Bruner suggests, is one by-product of the "cognitive revolution" in psychology: the readiness with which increased expertise in abstract, technically oriented thinking has been equated with development, perhaps to the detriment of narrative and artistic modes of elaboration. Rather than merely echoing values prominent in the culture, developmental theorists should enter as vigorous participants in the debate about the next generation.

Carol Gilligan, too, urges an alternative to the familiar controversy between moral monism and moral relativism or nihilism by urging the recognition of two distinct moral orientations that are inherent in the structure of human connection. One, the justice orientation, emphasizes the autonomy of the self and an ethic of fairness to other autonomous selves. This justice orientation has dominated the psychology of moral development almost to the exclusion of the other orientation, the caring orientation, which emphasizes the interdependence of persons and an ethic of compassion. The domination of justice over care, Gilligan maintains, is tied to the association of the orientations with gender and to methods that exclude women's views from study and that pull for justice considerations. Those manifestations of the caring orientation that survive have been mistakenly demoted to a developmentally lower status, thus confounding orientation and stage. Remapping moral development so as to include both orientations without subordinating one to the other will better represent human experience.

Turning to the presuppositions regarding terms and procedures that guide the empirical work of social scientists, Jerome Kagan defends five controversial assumptions against alternatives, relying on data as a guide to the usefulness of the assumptions. Kagan argues for descriptions that are specific rather than so general as to mute the effects of context; for categorical differences and discontinuities in functioning rather than an exclusive preference for continua and connectedness; for the subordination of reports about phenomenal experience to an objective framework of explanation; for recognition of the role of biological maturation in psychological development without assuming that one can partition endogenous and exogenous influences; and for the absence of special goals or ideals in development though attending to the possibility that there are universal moral sentiments. Kagan believes that the values of most developmental psychologists derive from the deepest assumptions of our society—optimistic belief in progress toward an ideal, positivistic faith in lawfulness, and liberal preferences for gradual, continuous change.

Although Bernard Kaplan agrees with Kagan in rejecting immanent laws in history or ontogenesis, Kaplan maintains that all of us are developmental psychologists in that we continually evaluate changes and differences with respect to ideals and standards. He proposes a persuasive definition of developmental psychology as a policy science promoting the perfection of the individual. According to this proposal, conceptual and empirical inquiry ought to work toward clarifying the telos of development and toward realizing the telos. Because cultural groups and, ultimately, individuals appear to take their own standards as transcendent while condemning the standards of others as parochial, both relativism and the possibility of a value-free descriptive science might seem appealing. However, because facts are made and not given, they depend on categories, methods, and language—including value distinctions—that may be alien to those studied. Thus, argues Kaplan, there can be no value-neutral description. Perfection of this line of thinking, as perfection of the concept of development, is taken by Kaplan to be a principle regulating theoretical activity, an ideal to be sought.

Marx Wartofsky joins in insisting that developmental psychology contributes to creating norms of development and goes further to claim that by so doing it influences how children, and the rest of us, do in fact develop. Historically, the construction of norms of development has taken place within three models of development: the essentialist conception that development is the actualization of fixed and inherent potentialities; the evolutionary conception that development is self-transforming through genetic and cultural adaptation; and the cultural-historical conception that development is self-constituting and self-transcending. In this last conception, activity pursued to realize represented human needs itself occasions new ends. Theorists of development have the responsibility to criticize the norms of development in society at large and in their own normative proposals. The theory of child development should be taken as a branch of social ethics or of critical social theory.

As diverse as they are, these contributors share in the conviction stated by Karl Mannheim (1954): "A clear and explicit avowal of the implicit metaphysical presuppositions which underlie and make possible empirical knowledge will do more for the clarification and advancement of research than a verbal denial of the existence of these presuppositions accompanied by their surreptitious admission through the back door" (p. 90).

REFERENCES

Kaplan, A. (1964). *The conduct of inquiry*. San Francisco: Chandler.

MacIntyre, A. (1978). Objectivity in morality and objectivity in science. In H. T. Engelhardt, Jr. & D. Callahan (Eds.), *Morals, science, and sociality* (pp. 21–39). Hastings-on-Hudson, NY: Hastings Center.

Mannheim, K. (1954). *Ideology and Utopia*. (L. Wirth & E. Shils, Trans.) New York: Harcourt. (Original work published 1929)

Weber, M. (1949). *The methodology of the social sciences* (E. A. Shils & H. A. Finch, Eds. and Trans.) Glencoe, IL: The Free Press. (Original work published 1904, 1905, 1917)

1 The Question of Moral and Social Development

Richard J. Bernstein
Haverford College

There is a deep paradox and anxiety in our contemporary discourse about the very concept of human development—especially as it pertains to moral and social development. On the one hand, we live in a time when there has been a flourishing of theories of human development, when many social scientists believe that we can base theories of development on empirical observations, elaborate sophisticated methodologies for testing hypotheses and theories, and advance our scientific understanding of human development that is free from ideological bias. But on the other hand, there is a widespread skepticism and questioning of the very idea of moral and social development. The multifaceted critique seeks to cut deeper than raising objections and criticisms about specific theories that have been advanced, but to question and deconstruct the very idea of human development—to show that although it is embedded in Western philosophic and scientific modes of thinking, the concept is suspect, for it is based on metaphysical assumptions that are dubious. Underlying this paradox is a growing anxiety. For any cool observer of the human condition in the latter part of the 20th century, it is difficult to resist the conclusion that the most probable telos of the human species is total self-annihilation, that despite all the talk of moral and social development, there seems to be an almost "ineluctable" logic working itself out leading to global disaster—a "logic" that appears to be happening to us, and over which no one has control. And this growing apprehension is reflected in a cultural anxiety, which I shall call the *Cartesian Anxiety*. This is the belief that *either* we can discover some solid foundation, some Archimedean point to ground a concept of human development, *or* we are confronted with intellectual and moral chaos, where "anything goes." There are a growing number of voices telling us that this state of radical relativism and nihilism is precisely our situation today.

I want to probe this paradox and anxiety. First I want to indicate how deep and pervasive the concept of human development has been in the tradition of Western thought; then consider some of the themes in the critique of this concept; finally I want to turn to how we might reconstruct and think about human development in our contemporary situation and historical horizon.

Conceptions of human development became manifest as soon as thinkers began to reflect on the question, what is the nature of the human species (typically what is man?)? They are already present in the Pre-Socratic thinkers. And by the time of classical Greek philosophy, most of the themes and motifs that have influenced subsequent theories of human development were well entrenched. Think of the powerful metaphors and tropes in Plato's *Dialogues*—the divided line, the allegory of the cave, the image of education as a turning and journey of the soul. There is directionality, a telos, structural stages of progression, a belief that although we live in a world of shadows, we can make the transition to reality, a transition by which we can become virtuous and approximate the Good. And this conception of human development—becoming what we truly are—encompasses what we would today call our cognitive, affective, and moral character. It is essentially holistic and has educational and political consequences, for it provides a standard for what must be done to cultivate a virtuous life, and enables us critically to assess any political community—judging it by the degree to which it fosters or inhibits human flourishing.

Despite the many important differences between Plato and Aristotle, the idea of human development is extended and deepened by Aristotle. Almost everything he wrote is influenced by his biological extension of the concept of development. It underlies and shapes his metaphysics, his psychology, his analysis of knowledge—as one moves from sensation, memory, imagination, experience, art, and science. Indeed, Aristotle's entire metaphysics is elaborated from a developmental perspective in which the concepts of potentiality and actuality are fundamental. And, of course, this sets the framework for his *Ethics* and *Politics*. Recently, Alasdair MacIntyre (1981) succinctly stated the moral scheme that underlies this way of thinking—a way of thinking that he takes to be characteristic of what he calls "the tradition of the virtues"—a tradition that had its origins long before classical Greek philosophy and lasted through the Middle Ages.

> There is a fundamental contrast between man-as-he-happens-to-be and man-as-he-could-be-if-he-realized-his-essential nature. Ethics is the science which is to enable men to understand how they make the transition from the former state to the latter. Ethics therefore on this view presupposes some account of potentiality and act, some account of the human *telos*. . . . We thus have a threefold scheme in which human-nature-as-it-happens-to-be (human nature in its untutored state) is initially

discrepant and discordant with the precepts of ethics and needs to be transformed by the instruction of practical reason and experience into human nature-as-it-could-be-if-it-realized-its-*telos*. (p. 50)

Now it is important to emphasize what this scheme presupposes. For it presupposes that there *is* a human nature, that we can *know* what it is, that there is a human telos, that we have the potential to actualize this telos, and that there are practical procedures for realizing or approximating it. As we shall see, every one of these presuppositions has been called into question.

MacIntyre (1981) claims that with the rise of "modernity," with what he calls "the Enlightenment project," this moral scheme was abandoned. Furthermore, he argues that the Enlightenment project of "rationally justifying" morality failed, and *had* to fail, resulting in a catastrophe "where people now think, talk and act *as if* emotivism were true, no matter what their avowed theoretical standpoint may be" (p. 21).

But for all the explicit criticism of a classical conception of human nature and teleology, something like this scheme has been appropriated, modified, and transformed by most modern thinkers, and indeed has served as the metaphysical underpinning of contemporary social scientific theories of moral and social development. Thus, for example, Hume and Kant, despite their distance from classical thought and the differences between them, are concerned to tell us what human nature and rationality really are. They are committed to a threefold scheme in which we can distinguish human nature in its untutored state, a telos or ideal of what we might become if we realized what we truly are, and with establishing a set of precepts for achieving this telos. Of course, we can realize with the aid of historical hindsight how, despite the perennial philosophic aspiration to achieve universal and ahistorical knowledge (episteme), their "visions" of human nature and its development are deeply influenced by historical and cultural prejudgments and biases. Indeed it should be sobering to realize how in every age (including our own) conceptions of human development have been advanced making the claim to universal validity, which turn out to be projections of historically situated cultural ideals. Thinkers in every age claim that *now* (for the first time) methods and procedures have been discovered for distinguishing genuine episteme (scientific knowledge) from mere opinion (doxa).

But although modern thinkers such as Hume and Kant appropriate a great deal from the traditions they are reacting against, they also sow the seeds for skepticism about this moral scheme of development. This becomes apparent in the famous passage from Hume's *Treatise* (1969) when he writes:

In every system of morality, which I have hitherto met with, I have always remarked, that the author preceeds for some time in the ordinary way of reasoning, and establishes the being of God, or makes observations concerning human affairs; when of a sudden I am surpriz'd to find, that instead of the usual copulations of propositions, *is* and *is not,* I meet with no proposition that is not connected with an *ought,* or an *ought* not. This change is imperceptible; but is, however, of the last consequence. For as this *ought,* or *ought not,* expresses some new relation or affirmation 'tis necessary that it should be observ'd and explain'd; and at the same time that a reason should be given, for what seems altogether inconceivable, how this new relation can be a deduction from others, which are entirely different from it. (p. 521)

Every subsequent theory of morality and moral development has had to confront the problem that Hume locates here. Kant sought to turn this fissure of the "is" and the "ought" into a philosophic virtue—arguing that a moral categorical "ought" can never be grounded in a posteriori claims about what "is" but only by appealing to a priori practical reason. Neither Hume nor Kant—nor most Enlightenment thinkers—seriously doubted that there is an objective and universal foundation for morality. For all Hume's skepticism about the *rational* foundations of morality, he argued that there are universal moral *sentiments* shared by all human beings. But the fissure introduced here was soon perceived as a major chasm.

One response to this "split" was that made by Hegel and Marx. Both relentlessly criticized the split between the "is" and the "ought." With Hegel, humanity itself was to be understood in the context of the dialectical development of *Geist* that diremps itself and overcomes (*Aufhebung*) itself in the course of its *historical* development. No longer is human development localized; it is universalized into a grand cosmic process. It is not surprising that Hegel (and Marx too) so deeply admired Aristotle, for both, in radically different ways, not only sought to overcome the modern dichotomy of the "is" and the "ought" but to reclaim the concepts of potentiality and actuality for understanding the historical teleological development of humanity. For all the apparent irrationality of history, both argue that there is a deeper dynamic logos at work leading to the concrete embodiment of human freedom. And both claim (with different understandings) that the time is at hand when we can grasp this dialectical developmental process by *Wissenschaft* (science).

Although the theoretical self-confidence of Hegel and Marx is gone, and our age is one that is profoundly fallibilistic, many contemporary theories of development stand in their shadow. When Kohlberg wrote his famous article "From is to Ought: How to Commit the Naturalistic Fallacy and Get Away with it in the Study of Moral Development," he rightly perceived *the* problem that any adequate theory of moral development must face. It makes good sense that one of Kohlberg's heroes is John Dewey, who himself attempted to scale down Hegel's grandiose claims, but appropriated from Hegel a historical developmental perspective.

But there has been another response to the fissure of the "is" and the "ought." The most dramatic representative is Nietzsche. The voices of Hegel, Marx, or even Dewey have become fainter in our time. They seem to be drowned out with variations on Nietzschean themes. Nietzsche's critique becomes so radical that the very idea of human development is called into question.

There are three interrelated themes suggested by Nietzsche that I want to consider. The first is his counter-discourse—his ironical narrative of moral and social development; his interpretation of the history of European civilization as a story of decline; his "unmasking" of morality as founded on *resentment;* the second is his claim that the idea of a determinate human nature is itself a fiction that tells us more about our grammatical categories and language than it does about any underlying reality; and the third is his questioning of truth and the will to truth.

Against the Enlightenment conviction that the history of the human species is one of progressive emancipation through use of reason and the extension of scientific knowledge, Nietzsche is one of the first to reveal "the dark side" of the dialectic of the Enlightenment. In this "hermeneutics of suspicion" he seeks to show that contrary to the manifest belief in furthering human autonomy, the history of Western civilization leads to nihilism.

He concludes his *Genealogy of Morals* (Nietzsche, 1969) by telling us:

> We can no longer conceal from ourselves *what* is expressed by all that willing which has taken its direction from the ascetic ideal: this hatred of the human, and even more of the animal, and more still of the material, this horror of the senses, of reason itself, this fear of happiness and beauty, this longing to get away from all appearance, change, becoming, death, wishing, from longing itself all this means—let us dare to grasp it—a *will to nothingness.* (p. 162–163)

But how is one to understand Nietzsche's own discourse? Is it intended to be a "true" narrative? But truth itself and the will to truth (which is only another variation of the ascetic ideal) require a critique—"The value of truth must for once be experimentally *called into question"* (Nietzsche, 1969, p. 153). And indeed Nietzsche not only critiques the will to truth, but is constantly trying to show us that we never break out of our metaphors, illusions, interpretations, and constructs—that every attempt to characterize human nature and human development is itself metaphorical. We desperately seek some "metaphysical comfort," to know the true essence of what we are, and yet if there is any "message" in Nietzsche, it is that we must learn to live without such comfort. Nietzsche (Kaufman, 1954) carries his critique to the most radical extreme when he writes:

> What then is truth? A mobile army of metaphors, metonyms and anthropomorphisms—in short a sum of human relations, which have been enhanced, transposed and embellished poetically and rhetorically, and which after long use seem firm, canonical and obligatory to a people: truths are illusions about which one has forgotten that this is what they are; metaphors which are worn out and without sensuous power; coins which have lost their pictures and now matter only as metal, no longer as coins. (pp. 46–47)

Nietzsche's "claims" may strike us as so extreme, so outrageous, so "irrational," that we may be tempted simply to dismiss them. Yet if we are honest we must at least recognize how influential he has been, how he speaks to many contemporary thinkers, how much of contemporary thought seems to be playing out variations on Nietzschean themes. We hear the reverberations in Weber, Horkheimer and Adorno, Heidegger, Foucault, Derrida, Feyerabend and Rorty (among many others). Let me briefly consider the working out of these Nietzschean themes in two thinkers who have special relevance for thinking about moral and social development: Weber and Foucault.

Weber's relation to the Enlightenment tradition is deeply ambivalent. For he was at once a rationalist who himself questioned the progressivist and emancipatory aspirations of the Enlightenment, and a passionate moralist who increasingly came to believe that there could be no rational foundation for our ultimate moral norms. He sought to work out with extraordinary comprehensiveness the progressive "rationalization" of Western society and the consequent disenchantment of the world. For the triumph of the mentality of *zweckrationalität*—instrumental or means-end rationality—affects and infects every domain of human life.[1] Weber accepts the Kantian dichotomy of the "is" and the "ought"—but his understanding of the ought side of this dichotomy is more Nietzschean than Kantian. He thought that science itself—to which he committed his life—was meaningless *in the sense* that it cannot give any answer to the question, "what shall we do and how shall we live?" The disenchantment of the world brought about by progressive rationalization destroys the traditional bases for moral and political orientations and traditional world views. And there is no turning back from this predicament. There is nothing that can lessen the burden and responsibility of choosing among the plurality of "gods" or "demons" that we decide to follow. Even Weber's "ethics of responsibility" is increasingly called into question when we realize the void that is at the center of our being. For Weber this is not just an individual or personal predicament. He was skeptical that any form of modern society could be successful in extricating us from the "iron cage" of bureaucratic "rationalization." What happens to the concept of human moral development from a Weberian perspective? One is tempted to say that it becomes an illusion—at least insofar as we believe that we can ground moral standards or principles in rational discourse. The "highest" stage of moral development is one in which we can live without illusions and recognize the groundlessness of all ultimate norms.

Initially the intellectual "distance" between Weber and Foucault seems to be enormous. Despite Weber's ambivalence to the Enlightenment tradition, we can still place him in this tradition. He is still very much a "modern" thinker—sharing and at the same time questioning many of the assumptions of modern

---

[1]Weber's view on rationality are much more complex than my brief treatment indicates. See the recent detailed examination of Weber in Habermas (1981).

thought. But the turn Foucault takes is much more extreme and radical. Yet we can read Foucault as complementing and extending Weber's analysis. And we can recognize their affinity in their common indebtedness to Nietzsche.

Like Nietzsche, Foucault's own appropriation of "genealogy" is intended to unmask and deconstruct—to show the historical background of "power of normalization and the formation of knowledge in modern society" (Foucault, 1979, p. 308). He thinks that Nietzsche was right in detecting how underlying and pervading the will to knowledge and truth is *power*. But his own analysis of knowledge/power differs from Nietzsche and Weber. Power is not centralized, repressive, or simply negative. It is all pervasive, capillary, and productive. Foucault (cited in Sheridan, 1980) tells us:

> When I think of the mechanics of power, I think of its capillary form of existence, of the extent to which power seeps into the very grain of individuals, reaches right into their bodies, permeates their gestures, their posture, what they say, how they learn to live and work with other people. (p. 217)

At first, it may seem that the "history" of madness, the "birth" of the clinic and the prison, and the "history" of sexuality are only marginal or peripheral to understanding modern society. But what Foucault is seeking to show us is that what first appears to be marginal is far more revealing about the micro-practices that form themselves into larger networks than the universals and global abstractions that have been central for philosophy and the human social sciences. It is in localized and specific ways that disciplinary techniques were evolved and refined in prisons, hospitals, psychiatric institutions, and schools—techniques that cohere and spread into larger networks and knowledge/power regimes.

When Foucault speaks of knowledge, truth, and power he wants to bracket all questions about their normative or epistemic legitimacy. He hypothesizes that " 'truth' is linked in a circular relation with systems of power which produce and sustain it, and to the effects of power which it induces and which extend it" (Foucault, 1980, p. 133). There is no "knowledge" and "truth" without its distinctive modality of power, and no power without its sustaining form of knowledge.

Ever since the publication of *Discipline and Punish,* Foucault has been concerned to describe in minute detail the specific techniques of control, individuation, and efficiency that were first marginally evolved, but have coalesced to transform modern society. Modern humanism, the "invention" of the human subject, and the emergence of the human and social sciences have all contributed to this new regime of power/knowledge that Foucault labels "the disciplinary society," "the carceral archipelago," "the panoptic society" where it is no longer even intelligible to speak of individuals, groups, or classes dominating or exercising power over others. Rather, the new mechanisms of discipline have a life and logic of their own. His "portrait" of modern society can be seen as the underside and microanalysis of the progressive triumph of *zweckrationalität* that Weber outlined. It is an illusion to think that modern humanism or the emergence of the human social sciences are really counterforces to the spread of disciplinary techniques. For example, he (Foucault, 1979) tells us:

> I am not saying that the human sciences emerged from the prison. But if they have been able to be formed and to produce so many profound changes in the *episteme,* it is because they have been conveyed by a specific and new modality of power: a certain policy of the body, a certain way of rendering the group of men docile and useful . . . the carceral network constituted one of the armatures of this power-knowledge that made the human sciences historically possible. (p. 305)

If we ask, what are the consequences of Foucault's inquiries for the very notion of human development? we can say that he calls into question both the concept of the "human" and "development." Both concepts are constructs that are only properly understood when we locate the grids, the discursive practices, the epistemes in which they are embedded. And against the Enlightenment conviction that there is a form of human and social knowledge that can further human emancipation, Foucault is constantly seeking to expose this "illusion" and to show the role that the human sciences play in fostering the spread and "legitimacy" of "the disciplinary society."

I have touched on only a few of the unsettling themes involved in the contemporary skeptical discourse about the concept of moral and social development. Hovering in the background of this discourse is radical relativism, a relativism that has spread from a concern with moral, social, and political issues, to the understanding of rationality, truth, knowledge, and science.

Listen to what Paul Feyerabend (1978) tells us:

> Reason is no longer an agency that directs other traditions, it is a tradition in its own right with as much (or as little) claim to the centre of the stage as any other tradition. Being a tradition it is neither good nor bad, it simply is. The same applies to all traditions—they are neither good nor bad, they simply are. They become good or bad (rational/irrational; pious/impious; advanced/'primitive'; humanitarian/vicious; etc.) only when looked at from the point of view of some other tradition. 'Objectively' there is not much to choose between anti-semitism and humanitarianism. But racism will appear vicious to a humanitarian while humanitarianism will appear vapid to a racist. *Relativism* (in the old simple sense of Protagoras) gives an adequate account of the situation which thus emerges. (pp. 8–9)

And although a philosopher like Richard Rorty (1982) appears to be more moderate in his claims, and seeks to diffuse the question of relativism, it is sometimes difficult to see how his own radical anti-foundationism, his claim that there is no "*privileged vocabulary,* the vocabulary which gets to the essence of the object, the one which expresses the properties which it has in itself as opposed to those which we read into it'' (Rorty, 1982, p. 152) differs substantially from what Feyerabend is telling us.

I do not think there is a facile way of answering this multifaceted critique of the concept of human moral and social development that I have characterized as variations on Nietzschean themes. Indeed, I think the question that needs to be probed is why so many contemporary thinkers are drawn to them. In part, I think this can be related to the "Cartesian Anxiety." For what is so characteristic of our times is the growing apprehension that there are no stable foundations, no Archimedean point, no basic constraints—where we are in a situation that Descartes (1969) metaphorically described as the fear of having "all of a sudden fallen into very deep water where 'I can neither make certain of setting my feet on the bottom, nor can I swim and so support myself on the surface' " (p. 149). Neither God, Philosophy, Science, or any cultural discipline answers to this "foundational" need.

But for all the rhetorical excesses of these critiques, there is also a great deal to be learned and appropriated from them. They teach us to be wary of the value presuppositions that are built into any theory of human moral and social development. They highlight the dangers of universalizing and hypostatizing what may only be well entrenched cultural ideals. They caution us to be skeptical that social scientific research can succeed in accomplishing what philosophic theories of human development have failed to achieve. They can make us much more aware of the ideological distortions and "structural violence" built into many theories of development. For theories of moral and social development have been ethnocentric, logocentric, and phallocentric. They frequently dignify and "legitimize" deeply embedded biases—as if they were "universal truths." We have to learn this lesson again and again—as we are now learning it from the feminist critiques and deconstruction of prevailing theories of development. But is there a way of learning from and appropriating these "truths," and reconstructing the concept of moral and social development? Can we escape the *aporias* of the fluctuation between objectivism and radical relativism which is so characteristic of our contemporary situation? For although these extremes still structure so much of contemporary discourse, I do believe something else is happening, that there is a questioning of the entire framework of thinking where these appear to be the only viable alternatives, that there is a growing sense of the need to *exorcise* the Cartesian Anxiety. And I also think there is a greater convergence and coherence in this movement beyond objectivism and relativism than is apparent in what sometimes seems like a competing babble of voices. I cannot adequately justify these claims here, but I want to give some indications and tentative suggestions of what I mean.[2]

---

[2]These are the issues that I explore in my book, *Beyond Objectivism and Relativism* (Bernstein, 1983).

One converging result of many lines of contemporary thought is to make us profoundly aware of our historicity, finitude, and fallibility. We are beings who are constituted by our traditions, social practices, our funded prejudgments. As Gadamer and MacIntyre tell us, we are always being effectively shaped by the traditions that are the source of our historical and social identities. This does not mean that our appropriation of a tradition need be one of uncritical acceptance. "Traditions, when vital, embody continuities of conflict" (MacIntyre, 1981, p. 206). Traditions and inherited social practices are not monolithic. But it is an illusion to believe that we can escape our historicity—an illusion by which *both* objectivists and radical relativists are tempted. This is a lesson or "truth" that is even reinforced by the post-empiricist philosophy and history of science. But although our thinking and reasoning is always situated in historical changing social practices, it is also projective and anticipatory. We are, as the pragmatic thinkers have taught us, always *in medias res*. There are not absolute origins or finalities. When we speak about moral and social development in the sense of what we and our fellow human beings may yet become, we always *project* some ideal, some vision—a vision that derives its power from our understanding of our history and its prospects. We need to recognize that there are a plurality of narratives that we can tell about ourselves and a plurality of visions we can project. But pluralism is not radical relativism. For if we take our historicity seriously, then we cannot escape giving the best possible reasons and arguments for our interpretations—fully realizing our fallibility. We never escape the situation of what Gadamer calls hermeneutical understanding and Charles Taylor calls "interpretive dialectics" where we seek to persuade by the overall *plausibility* of our interpretations.[3] And we need to recognize that there are no algorithmic decision procedures or methods by which we can definitely evaluate competing interpretations. But this does not mean that evaluating the plausibility of competing interpretations is merely arbitrary or idiosyncratically subjective. Rather it means we must recognize that rational evaluation is more flexible, open, situated than the Cartesian dream would lead us to believe.

I not only believe we are coming to a more realistic and intellectually modest way of thinking about moral and social development, but there are many indications of the emergence of a common shared vision—even among those who at first seem to sharply disagree with each other. For many independent lines of inquiry keep gravitating toward the themes of the need to reclaim and nurture communication oriented toward mutual understanding, dialogue, and conversation.

This is one of the most dominant themes in our own pragmatic tradition. It is boldly announced by Peirce in his emphasis on the "community of inquirers," explored from a social-psychological perspective by Mead, and extended by John Dewey who perceived that the greatest threat of the twentieth century is the

---

[3]See the discussion of "interpretive dialectics" in Charles Taylor (1975).

breakdown of genuine communal life. It is reiterated in the "pragmatism" of Richard Rorty (1982) when he defends what he calls the "Socratic virtues"— "the willingness to talk, to listen to the people to weigh the consequences of our actions upon other people" and when he calls for a "renewed sense of community" (p. 166).

Rorty (1982) continues:

> Our identification with our community, our society, our political tradition, our intellectual heritage—is heightened when we see this community as *ours* rather than nature's, *shaped* rather than *found,* one among many which men have made. In the end, the pragmatists tell us, what matters is our loyality to other human beings clinging together against the dark, not our hope of getting things right. (p. 166)

But this theme also emerges from the phenomenological and hermeneutical tradition, especially in the thinking of Gadamer and Ricoeur. One way of grasping the turn that hermeneutics has taken in them is to see that they are telling us that we are essentially dialogical beings—always engaged in open conversation where we must always be prepared to risk and test our prejudgments and prejudices. Gadamer (1981) is always scanning the horizon to reclaim and rediscover "those solidarities that could enter into a future society of humanity" (p. 87). And when he seeks to summarize what is meant by practice (*praxis*), he tells us "Practice is conducting oneself and acting in solidarity. Solidarity, however, is the decisive condition land basis of all social reason" (Gadamer, 1981, p. 87).

And despite the long debate that Habermas has had with the hermeneutical tradition and with Gadamer, the theme of the centrality of undistorted communication and the ideal of communicative action-oriented intersubjective reciprocal understanding, shared knowledge and mutual trust are what lie at the center of his own vision of moral and social development. His disagreement with Gadamer is not about the centrality of dialogue and communicative rationality as a regulative ideal, but about the analysis of those structural features of contemporary society that distort and obstruct its realization.

Even Alasdair MacIntyre (1981) gives expression to this vision, when he concludes his despairing analysis of our contemporary moral situation by calling for "the construction of local forms of community within which civility and the intellectual and moral life can be sustained through the new dark ages which are already upon us" (p. 245).

Indeed I think that there are signs that even post-structuralist French thinkers like Foucault and Derrida are pursuing a dialectic that leads us to a similar vision.

I do not want to suggest that all these intellectual movements and voices are saying the same thing. They are not. Nor do I want to suggest that the differences among them are less consequential than anything that they share in common. But I do think, however tentative and groping, what is emerging is a new way of thinking about moral and social development and a widely shared common vision of the need to foster the telos of dialogical communities that may yet serve to orient our praxis.

There is no dearth of pessimistic analyses of our contemporary social situation and totalizing critiques that end in despair. There is wide-spread cynicism about even the possibility of any social reform that does not have its dark side. But it is also true that there are counter tendencies, that there are deep urges and needs for solidarity, community, sharing, and reciprocal understanding. It is these fragile experiences that must be preserved and fostered if we want to keep alive the very idea of moral and social development.

REFERENCES

Bernstein, R. (1983). *Beyond objectivism and relativism: Science, hermeneutics, and praxis*. Philadelphia: University of Pennsylvania Press.

Descartes, R. (1969). *Meditations: The philosophical works of Descartes* (Vol. I). Cambridge: Cambridge University Press.

Feyerabend, P. (1978). *Science in a free society*. London: New Left Books.

Foucault M. (1979). *Discipline and punish*. New York: Vintage Books.

Foucault, M. (1980). Truth and power. In C. Gordon (Ed.), *Power/knowledge*. New York: Pantheon Books.

Gadamer, H. G. (1981). *Reason in the age of science*. Cambridge, MA: MIT Press.

Habermas, J. (1981). *Theorie des kommunikativen handelns*. Frankfurt: Suhrkamp Verlag.

Hume, D. (1969). *A treatise of human nature*. Baltimore: Penguin Books.

Kaufmann, W. (1954). *The portable Nietzsche*. New York: Viking Press.

MacIntyre, A. (1981). *After virtue*. Notre Dame: University of Notre Dame Press.

Nietzsche, F. (1969). *On the genealogy of morals* (W. Kaufmann, Trans.) New York: Vintage Books.

Rorty, R. (1982). Pragmatism, relativism, and irrationalism. Also Nineteenth Century idealism and Twentieth Century textualism. In *Consequences of pragmatism*. Minneapolis: University of Minnesota Press.

Sheridan, A. (1980). *Michel Foucault: The will to truth*. London: Tavistock.

Taylor, C. (1975). *Hegel*. Cambridge: Cambridge University Press.

DISCUSSION

BRUNER: I just want to make a statement: Bravo! [Applause]

KAPLAN: Can I ask a question? Any statements that Foucault or others claim to be true—are they also true qualified in some way? I'm raising the question of reflexivity. Very often, people say, "I make an absolute statement that. . . ." I wonder whether you want to comment in some way about this issue: All these claims that Gadamer makes, that Ricoeur makes, are they also local, parochial, historical, not true, or true in some qualified way?

BERNSTEIN: The question calls to mind several things I want to speak about. What's interesting to me about arguments concerning relativism is their remarkable continuity. After all, on the one hand the argument against relativism, the self-referential argument, is as old as philosophy itself. We find it in Plato. Relativists are never convinced by that kind of argument. On the other hand, the so-called objectivists always make the remark, "Well, maybe this foundation cracked, but the idea itself is not suspect so we have to begin anew." That's a typical stance of almost every modern philosopher: We must begin anew.

Now it does seem to me that several things have happened in modern discourse. One is that these types of arguments have spread way outside questions of moral and social development. We can trace the movement from the 19th century to what is so fashionable today—to call into question rationality, truth, norms, etc.

Now, there are strategies by which so-called relativists can defend themselves against this type of objection. But what I think is more important is this itself reflects a framework of thinking: That you claim that in the end these are the only two viable alternatives. What I see now taking place is a questioning of the whole framework of these alternatives: Objectivism versus relativism. If you question this, we never escape the demand for giving reasons and arguments, [but] they simply do not have the conclusiveness of the dream of deductive proof or empirical verification as was classically formulated. If you recognize that every interesting argument is always going to be flexible, always going to be situated, always going to be in some ways open to a kind of counter-argument, then, from my point of view, it begins to shift the issue. It shifts the issue to a practical question. How do you foster communities in which we're not just simply trying to manipulate, but we're trying to do the best we can to persuade each other, recognizing that there is a *rational* kind of persuasion?

That's the sub-text, or the sub-structure, of what seems to me emerging from very different lines of thinking. I think there has been a great deal of mystification in the philosophy of science which discusses the issue as if it were a matter of objectivism or relativism, and that's not what I think we're discovering. I think we're discovering that science itself is less algorithmic than the dream has been of many scientists and philosophers.

KAPLAN: Maybe I haven't been clear.

BERNSTEIN: There are two ways of answering questions: to answer them or to say something else that you want to say. [Laughter]

KAPLAN: I was thinking about something like this: If you say that things have been mystified, or anybody says things have been mystified, presumably there is a standard against which mystification is judged. If you say that it is true that this is happening today, do you use a standard of truth? Those who criticize—are they themselves subtly invoking what they criticize in the process of making their statements?

BERNSTEIN: I would want to say yes, but it isn't quite what you think. Take the example that you began with. Foucault is doing his analysis and saying that something is wrong, something is mystification. There is clearly an implicit appeal that his form of discourse is more illuminating, more perspicuous, and so forth. Okay. The next move is where there is danger. "Ah-ha, I got you! If you're doing it, then let's get out your theory of truth; let's get out the kind of basic discourse." That's been a standard move which I think is increasingly called into suspicion. I think that any serious discourse—whatever terms we want to use, whether it be truth, whether it be illumination, whether it be insight—is making that kind of claim. But I think it's too easy and too facile to say, "Ah-ha, that'll commit you to some kind of basic conception of truth, and then you're no better off than that which you are criticizing." I think that that doesn't quite follow.

BRUNER: I want to take my text in response to this from Foucault's *The Archeology of Knowledge*. The point that I want to make is this: It is indeed the case that the very statement of a canon of criticism creates with it a reality, a set of presuppositions concerning its base and, once accepted, produces what might be called a conventional society that lives by it. The notion of deconstructionism, for example, is a popular, accepted, conventional view which is pushed to the extremes of something that I'll call for a moment, a "limit of convenience." You get a phenomenon which, in a sense, cleanses for a while. You get a community which is based essentially on negotiatory processes or hermeneutic processes and those somehow contribute to the culture.

But to go back to *The Archeology of Knowledge*. You remember his discussion of the extent to which a set of beliefs persists just by virtue of their existence, just by virtue of the fact that they had a kind of quasi-axiomatic structure. In the cultural realm it's a bit like Kuhn's paradigms in science; that is, they have a being because they build up a structure and that structure gets to be taken as conventional. I think the worry that the world will turn toward a radical relativism that will constantly bring into question each view as it comes up and lead to a kind of flux somehow does not fit with, as I see it, and indeed as Foucault sees, the flow of human intellectual and moral history. That is, in a sense, it has built into it a kind of pause point in which the culture conventionalizes and tries out, and the changes tend to be unpredictable, sharp. Yet, when looked at from a longer perspective, they were not quite as unpredictable and not as sharp as one thought.

BERNSTEIN: I tend to be sympathetic with what you just said. I am, in one way, more of a rationalist, not in the sense of believing that dream of philosophers or scientists that we can once and for all lay out the criteria of rationality, but (this is the significance of the point about historicity) we are beings committed to argumentation. We cannot escape it. This is where the objectivists and the relativists are on the same wavelength because the relativist talks as if you could simply leap out of the things that have shaped you, as if you could simply give up your claim to arguments. We can recognize their fallibility. We can recognize that their structures change. But (and this is where I'm sympathetic with what I would call the pragmatic version of Habermas) that appeal to argumentation is part of our historicity is nonescapable. In this sense, it does seem to me that radical relativism is just an illusion. It is healthy at certain points; it is necessary; but it is just [an illusion].

KAGAN: Let me make a plea for absolutes in this sea of relativism. I suggest that we will always ask what is best, because there is a part of our nature that is not historically conditioned in any way, that leads every three-year-old in every culture to want an answer to that question. The problem is that there are two bases for personal acceptance of what is right, and a chasm between them. One is what we feel is right, and the other is that which is deductively persuasive. The problem is that there is no way to assimilate one to the other. The relative argument is always based on a rational, never a sentimental, basis, but I believe in a sentimental basis. Hume was right: The basic human emotion is sympathy, what some call empathy, that cannot be taken out of our nature and cannot be translated into a deductive argument.

BERNSTEIN: On the last point, I absolutely agree. I'm a little bit more cautious about your other claims. After all, there are two ways of cutting this. The way in which I prefer to cut it is that there is something wrong with the traditional dichotomy between sentiment and reasoning.

KAGAN: What's wrong with it?

BERNSTEIN: Let me speak to the first issue and then go back to this. What Hume was confident about, at least in some of his moments, is that indeed there are universal sentiments. It seems to me that at least we have to be cautious about that.

KAGAN: Why are you skeptical?

BERNSTEIN: I'm skeptical because it is a question of whether the sentiments really are shaped by history. If we look at the history of ethics, that every culture has an ethical basis, that every culture makes distinctions of right and wrong is undeniable. That metapoint has to be conceded. But what is taken to be valuable? What is felt to be good? What is felt to be the proper kind of response? It seems to me that there is a good deal of variation from culture to culture, and, in that sense, Hume is not just making a formal point but a substantive point which I am dubious about.

On the other question that you asked me—I don't have time to develop this completely, but what I do see is that in the history of modern thought there has been a narrowing of the conception of rationality. There has been an instrumentalization of rationality. I think that Weber is right in seeing that for what became the dominant mode rationality is a kind of means-ends rationality which excludes the whole domain of feeling and sentiment. Well, after all, there have been in philosophy counter tendencies to this—a much more dynamic, much more passionate conception of reason. If I am right about what is happening now, we are beginning to become suspicious of instrumental forms of reasoning. Then we can recognize that there can be partisanship for reason, that it is in itself not something which is just pure. Then, it seems to me, the line between "sentiment" and rationality becomes blurred. That's the sense in which I would rather cut it the other way, rather than accept what has become a well-entrenched modern dogma.

WARTOFSKY: As you know from the past, I get a little impatient, even feisty, when I hear about this ideal of mutual dialogue, community, and agreement, because there are some things I don't want to have to come to agreement about with other people. Therefore, I'm not going to aim at any kind of a shared, mutual, reciprocal recognition of what we both agree on. There are going to be some things I'm going to utterly disagree about. So, I'm a little bit disturbed when the question of moral or social development takes as its new end or telos here this notion of shared mutual, reciprocal agreement. By the way, I don't like the way Gadamer takes over the word "solidarity." And Rorty's using it now too—I have a different historical background, and the word has very different connotations for me.

BERNSTEIN: Yes, I know. [Laughter]

WARTOFSKY: There are some mutualities which would be vicious to achieve. There is nothing I want to come to agreement about with a racist, regarding his racism, for example. Therefore, there may be something right about what you are saying methodologically, namely about the Socratic dialogue into which I enter; but it can't be extended either ontologically or epistemologically or morally (unless you want to talk about the morality of methods). Morally, epistemologically, and ontologically there are some things which are right and some things which are wrong, no matter how many people have come to agree one way or the other about it. So, we're back to the very old question of relativism. I don't want to put it this boldly but I'd like it answered because . . .

BERNSTEIN: Fine.

WARTOFSKY: I've been slithering between what I call the Scylla of essentialism and the Charybdis of historical relativism . . .

BERNSTEIN: So has everybody.

WARTOFSKY: . . . for a long time, trying not to get sucked into a whirlpool or smashed against a rock, but I'm not happy with the rather rosy view you present. When you say the "weak Habermasian position," I would rather think that the only saving grace for that position is Habermas' insistence that the norm of undistorted communication is counterfactual. It's not something one, in fact, intends to arrive at. It's proposed rather, as the kind of absolute or transcendental ideal towards which the discourse *ought* to tend, rather than an account of the discourse itself. But, in that sense, it has very much the same heuristic status as Descartes' conception of truth or Aristotle's notion of the good.

BERNSTEIN: I'm glad you asked the question because it's the inevitable question. But, first of all, let me just take a technical point. What I meant is this: that at times Habermas talks like what I'm calling an objectivist; at times he talks as if the ideal, the counterfactual, is built into intersubjectivity.

WARTOFSKY: But there is an appeal to some transcendental ground.

BERNSTEIN: Okay. I do not believe that argument really holds up. I believe he is giving, in the sense in which Charles Taylor would give, an *interpretation* of our history and our prospects showing that somehow this telos, this counterfactual, is built into what we are, and to try to escape it is to play games with ourselves. This *is* our historical project, and you can't just leap out of it; you can't deny that, in that sense, you have commitment.

But let me get to the main issue. I do not think that talk about undistorted communication, dialogue, and so forth, is intended to mean, in the American sense, consensus where all agree. You always have built into it the counterfactual, and what you are trying to do is relocate the nature of differences. It seems to me that as long as we are speaking about morals and political life there is always going to be plurality, and there is no way of escaping it. The key issue as I see it is how do you understand the plurality? Do you understand the plurality as irreconcilable positions where you have to then stop because you are either accepting some kind of emotivism or basic norm where there is no further court of appeal? Or, is there the possibility that although we may not come to agreement, at least come to an understanding of where we do disagree? I want to resuscitate the whole realm of opinion, of persuasiveness. We cannot find a decision procedure, but still, at least in the background, is the commitment to a certain kind of discourse. That's the direction in which I would like to go because what seems to me desperately wrong in so much contemporary discourse, whether it be Weberian or of other sorts, [is that] it has taken pluralism as a fundamental ontological fact from which there is nothing more to be said. And that, I think, is always wrong.

2

Value Presuppositions of Developmental Theory

Jerome Bruner
New School for Social Research

Like others participating in this Symposium, I quickly discovered that it was much too constricting and misleading besides to focus an essay on the value presuppositions of developmental theory upon the work of any one particular theorist. It was constricting for the good reason that any theory worth its salt derives one particular set of surface rules concerning human development from a more general deep structure from which many surface rules can be derived. And it is far better to consider developmental theory at the deeper, presuppositional level to examine why, perhaps, particular theories are derived as they are to emphasize one rather than another rule. To take an example, all theories must choose a particular way of dealing with the balance between, let us say, inner and outer determination of developmental change. Piaget (1952) deals with it as a resultant balance of the processes of assimilation and accommodation. Freud emphasizes a number of quite different processes—like the compromise of an earlier primary pleasure principle and a later secondary reality one, or the requirement of maintaining defenses that will both inhibit unacceptable impulses and yet permit their expression in a symptomatic if hidden manner. Werner (1948) is more complicated than either of the others and proposes that inner and outer determination operate jointly at all phases of growth, however syncretic, however lacking in overall integration.

The point is not whether each is "right" nor whether each proposes an adequate way of formulating the problem. Rather, it is that the real value question relates not to the mechanism proposed for integrating inner and outer processes, nor does it relate to how one chooses to balance the two in the outcome. It relates rather to the question of whether and how a particular theorist draws any ethical consequences from the distinction, whether for example "inner" is equated somehow (as with Freud and Piaget) with the primitive that "ought" to be expunged in the course of growth.

Before I start, however, I owe you an accounting of the biases that I bring to this task. I lean in an enterprise of this kind toward a very astringent linguistic skepticism. On such journeys as this one, I enjoy the company of such philosophers as Roger Wertheimer (1972) and John Austin (1962). I do not believe nor have I ever believed for a twinkling of an eye that you can in any way derive deontic propositions from epistemic ones, that there is no linguistic or logical way of going from propositions about what is or what exists to propositions that contain those three words that are the holy trinity of ethics: "ought," "good," and "right." It is not simply that Wertheimer has given such a convincingly devastating account of trying to distinguish between such expressions as "Children ought to love their parents" and "The steak ought to be ready in 5 minutes." That is pretty bad. But even worse is the historical hocus-pocus that has gone into trying to justify going from existential statements to value ones. As John Austin (1962) puts it (with almost burlesqued understatement), "It's rather a pity that people are apt to invoke a new use of language whenever they feel so inclined, to help them out of this, that, or the other well-known philosophical tangle." And nowhere has this been more evident than in efforts to justify the leap from the copula "is" to the modal "ought." I shall not pursue the matter here but refer you, rather, to Wertheimer's (1972) lively discussion of the many ways in which one can fall and many have fallen into the "naturalistic fallacy," as this derivation from the epistemic to the deontic is formally called.

All of which is *not* to say that theories of development *ought* not to take value positions about the course of human growth and development. Indeed, I would want to urge (a) that it is impossible not to take such positions and still be a developmental theorist, and (b) that the positions one takes provide a major selection principle for guiding the research one does. What I wish to make clear at the outset, however, is that I do not think "the facts" of human development by themselves tell you in any way, in not even the slightest way, what value positions one should take—whether it be that to achieve formal operations is better than halting at concrete ones, that it is better to cultivate "peak experiences" than to wallow about in ordinary ones, that where there was id there should now be ego. These are all *morally* justifiable positions that can be derived, no doubt, from suitably formulated value axioms. They simply have nothing to do with what one learns about the nature of formal operations, peak experiences, or ego functioning.

Why do I say then that a developmental theory is impossible without a base of valuational axioms? It is because I believe that in principle theories of human development constitute a *policy science,* a science whose intrinsic object is not simply to describe but to prescribe alternative optimal ways of achieving certain outcomes. This deep truth is frequently disguised (and well disguised at that) by choosing the growth patterns of particular children or of children in particular milieux and holding those patterns up as normal or, worse, as "natural," with the heavy implication that other patterns of growth are in some manner deviant. Let me argue, consonant with my claim about developmental theory being a policy science, that it also falls into the category of what Herbert Simon (1957) refers to as a "science of the artificial." For what is characteristic of our species is that we create the environments in which we live, not only technologically but, more importantly, symbolically. As sociologists like Berger and Luckmann (1966), anthropologists like Geertz (1973) and Sperber (1973), and psychologists like Heider (1958) and George Kelley (1955) have been urging for the last decade, we create an environment by the invocation of symbolic texts that stand as constituted realities. By the use of principally linguistic means—performatives, presuppositional loadings, and other pragmatic devices as well as by the use of myths and other ontic devices—we create an implicit world such as we think one *ought* to be. As Geertz puts it, we create public meanings to which we then insist upon adhering. When we are in doubt about the particulars, we negotiate explicit versions of implicit meanings. By linguistic means we constitute realities like "promises," and then we negotiate them into the explicit form of say, "contracts," which if violated will get you not only into symbolic trouble but into the bricks and mortar of a real-world jail.

A developmental theory (when it is a policy science) is a device for describing how to navigate in the value-laden and constructed world of symbols and technology created by the society for its own regulation. I had better explain now what I meant a moment ago by an *ontic device*. It is a term that I borrow from Carol Feldman (1974). She comments upon the fact that the results of certain cognitive processes are given canonical status as "realities." They are marked linguistically in an appropriate way and endowed with the sort of "exteriority and constraint" that Durkheim (1965) noted as characterizing deities and religious truths. The "truth" of science, for example, is given this kind of ontic status. The contrast class comprises conjectures and speculations and hypotheses that are still "in the head" rather than "in the world." Endowing the outputs of cognitive processes with ontic status, Feldman notes, serves other ends as well—as in problem solving when we endow a provisional but likely-seeming outcome with "reality" as a *given* and use it as the base for corrective reckoning, much as paradigms in science are used.

In any case, it is by some such device as "ontic dumping" that we stipulate that certain familiar development outcomes in familiar cultural settings have the brevet of being "natural" and, consequently, "desirable." Middle-class problem solving styles, male gender value systems, RP English, Stage VI moral reasoning, base-rate Bayesian judgment, ego autonomy, and self-directed competence—all have been taken as natural and desirable developmental outcomes for which, indeed, appropriate curricula or appropriate therapies could be devised. It should be no surprise, then, that writers like Kessen (1979) and Sheldon White (1976) have remarked that developmental research is in fact more often mounted as a way of justifying public policy toward children after the fact than as a means of formulating it beforehand. But even if it were used as an aid to the formulation of policies, it would still be marked in the same way, for policies do not grow from facts without the mediation of values.

Let me make one last preliminary point before turning to the case history that I want to present in demonstration of my point. It has to do with the role of the developmental psychologist as a participant in the debate over the "ought" where human development is concerned. I believe his or her role to be crucial on two scores, both of them critical for the conduct of a society and both of them extending well beyond the argument that informed citizens have a particularly responsible role. The first has to do with clarity concerning ends, the second with the clarification of means-end relationships.

It is sometimes the case that the aims a society cherishes for its children (however they may be framed in naturalistic language) may be contradictory. Such aims are as often implicit and in the form of maxims as they are explicitly formulated in policies for children. "We" (the society, the collectivity, the value makers, the school board, whatever) may wish children to be both inno-vatively creative in their problem solving and obedient to authority. It may, in fact, provide an impossible trade-off. The opportunity cost for inculcating obe-dience to authority may include not risking innovative solutions in the presence of authority, with the result that we encourage private daring and public banality among those growing up in a generation dominated by this dual and contradicto-ry ideal. Here I think that our knowledge and our findings locked up in inaccessi-ble form in our golden journals must have a special role in the debate.

So too in the matter of means-end confusions. Where, for example, policy makers believe that the best way to create family solidarity in the next generation is to assure at all costs and under all circumstances that children stay home with their mothers and, accordingly, create severe and damaging tensions among a sizable number of children and their mothers by failing to provide suitable care facilities, then plainly our research is relevant—though not always heeded, as I have learned most recently in Great Britain (Bruner, 1980).

Doctors do their thing by virtue of there being a wide consensus about the value of health. But even that is no longer so simple. Health for whom? The chances for beating the odds on infant mortality are better in the Northern Region of Nigeria than in Black Harlem. Lawyers did their thing (probably closer to our thing than what doctors do) by arguing they were in the cause of justice for all— until a distinguished group of legal lights a short time ago noted that they did so for the rich, not the poor. So even the constitutive realities of health and justice come up again for scrutiny and for negotiation and begin to lose their ontic obviousness.

And what about us, we in developmental theory?

Let me present my case history. It has to do, I suppose, with the "cognitive revolution" and the change in emphasis that it imposed upon developmental theory. Or more specifically, with the change in value implications that it imposed. As I have noted elsewhere in more detail, the cognitive revolution coincides roughly with that point in our history when, Peter Drucker (1955) assures us, about half of the gross national product was derived from industries and services having to do with the dissemination of information and knowledge, with management and control processes, with the design of systems that could produce intelligent and corrigible results, and so on. It also happened to be the take-off point for the development of computational automata that were superbly suited for dealing with well-formed problems by intelligent programs that simulated the activities of experts rather than novices. We even went so far as to create a major new ontic entity to honor the powers of the new devices: Artificial Intelligence.

The effect of all of this was to liberate us from mechanical models of human learning and to cleanse for polite use a four-letter word that, in the main, had before been taboo in polite psychological society: Mind. We first put Mind into machines, and that made it quite all right. It was all a bit reminiscent of cleansing Mafia money by depositing it in an unregistered but impeccable Swiss bank account.

See now what has happened. Quite without intending to do so, we have fallen into a set of new postures in developmental psychology—evaluational postures. In their way, they are admirable, as far as they go (at least from the point of view of my explicit value system which, I want to assure you again, derives from the logic of my passions rather than from any knowledge I have acquired through my research). The most striking example I can cite comes directly from the heartland of the new technology for the study of thought processes: from Herbert Simon's laboratory. It is the theory that human development can be likened to the transition that characterizes the passage from being a novice to being an expert. And it is impossible to deny that in certain respects, there is truth in this proposition. And indeed, it is verifiable as well that one can help a novice toward expertise by teaching him more expert heuristics and by giving him some indoctrination in that form of reflective mindfulness that we now call metacognition. All of this we can surely celebrate: It is a far cry beyond rote learning and reinforcement schedules for specific response patterns.

But mind the consequence. Look at the curious asymmetric bimodality that begins to emerge in our valuation of the outcomes of development. Let me mention a few: They all point in the direction of favoring by implicit endorsement those traits that promote expertise or, at least, do not interfere with it.

Take first the vulgarization of Piagetian theory. I say vulgarization, because Piaget and his colleagues never intended that their account of the development of intelligence be a complete description of all forms of mindfulness—especially the narrative, poetic, imaginative, metaphoric skill to which I want to return finally—nor of those social skills that have as their prime requisite that the problem solver take as fully as possible into account the social context in which action occurs and the stance of the various actors involved. His aim, rather, was to explore structural affinities in the growth of operational reasoning in the child that might account for the historical growth of mathematics, logic, and the natural sciences.

So just as science advanced through its initial preoccupation with the appearance of things and primitive, causal ideas based on the model of the human as an agent to the idea of systematicity based on invariant properties of a set of elements under transformation, with causality framed in terms of the structured outcome of the full set of possible interactions of the system as a whole, until finally it became possible to work with a formal model rather than directly on nature to obtain results, so too the child (in general) was seen to develop. I do not for a moment doubt that Piaget was well aware of the disanalogies involved between the history of the child and the history of science, and it was certainly his well-advised privilege to ignore them, given his broader interest in genetic epistemology.

But how eagerly we in the developed world (with notable exceptions) embraced these ideas as a *full* account of development! And how quickly we adapted our educational procedures to reproduce in little Everyman (we should better call her Everychild) the same developmental stages. I think the effects were unquestionably salubrious. Mind and thought were readmitted into education.

Modern, scientific mind. I am trying to recall whether there were any studies on what happens to artistic and narrative elaboration when the child moves from preoperational reasoning to the use of the *Viergruppe* and the Sixteen Binary Propositions in her reasoning? Is there loss in fantasy? Do the riches that Vivian Paley (1981) recounts in her *Wally's Stories* begin to recede as the child learns to ignore context in the interest of tracking invariance? Is the opportunity cost of accommodation to the world a loss in zest for creating rich and satisfying fantasy? Is there some way in which continued assimilation of the world to one's own inner structures can be assured while accommodation is being nurtured by the *aliment* of physical nature?

Please do not misunderstand me. I am not beleaguering Piagetian theory nor pillorying Herbert Simon. What I am arguing only is that culturally congruent phenomena unearthed or constructed by modern theories of human development come to be canonized as desirable realities if they conform to values already independently in being within the culture. Where theories of human development become classic, moreover, is when they unearth or discern a previously undiscovered grouping of processes that extend or elaborate a cultural value that was previously implicit and is now made explicit. In this sense, developmental theory is an arm of culture-creating. In that sense they are as Oscar Wilde said, an instance of life imitating art. They become part of the negotiatory process for making that which before was implicit into that which is now explicit.

But even short of classic, theories have a way of weighting their continua and contrasts such that they are marked for cultural acceptability and unacceptability—as in the examples I have already proposed. If I may caricature what I mean by an illustration from the domain of personality theory, I would take the distinction between impulsive and reflective. Reflectiveness automatically becomes the favored limb, impulsiveness suspect. Impulsivity is feminine, related to unconscious drives, disruptive of well-ordered plans, and it generates unpredictability. But folklore has it (and some tests as well, I daresay) that the fiery artistic temperament that goes with the writing of novels and poetry (a Kurt Vonnegut or Robert Lowell), the performance of great works of music and dance (you may choose your own examples according to taste), and even the generation of original discoveries in mathematics and logic (Godel and Wittgenstein will do), that impulsiveness in conjunction with high intelligence is associated with originality. How else could one take one's transient hunches seriously? If one argues in response to this point that "genius will out" or that there is not much sense in planning a society for the production of a small minority of inspired impulsives, or that you need predictability to keep the show on the road, I will perhaps agree—but not on the basis of anything epistemic within the theory or inherent in the data it might have generated. The claims are arbitrary with respect to science; they derive from value presuppositions.

Finally, let me sound a more substantive note concerning value presuppositions in modern theories of human development. I have already mentioned it in passing. There are at least two fundamentally different ways in which language is used and they either reflect a predisposition to use mind in certain ways or create the disposition once language becomes an instrument of thought. The one is, to use Jakobson's (1960) distinction, a horizontal axis of combination—what he calls the metonymic mode. Its principle linguistic instrument is the topic-comment structure and its formal expression is through predication. Its function is essentially narrative: to create stories and themes and accounts of what is related to what. It is sensitive to context, to the pragmatic stance of the narrator, to the uptake of interlocutors, to frame. Its ultimate structure lies in the structure of discourse and dialogue and story.

Its contrast is the metaphoric mode, the vertical axis of selection, in Jakobson's words. It is ordered by principles such as synonymy, hyponymy, hyperonymy, and at its most effective it achieves a comprehensive classificatory tree-structure. In natural language, it is nuanced in terms of nested sets of semantic markers that allow ordering by quality as well as by inclusion rules. In artificial languages, nuancing is usually tamed by reference to a more formal metric.

In the past, psychologists have recognized the two modes as syntagmatic and paradigmatic, terms that arose in connection with two different forms of word association: table-supper in contrast to, say, table-furniture. The syntagmatic or metonymic mode is constrained principally by the case-like nature of subject-predicate grammars, constrained in a semantic sense, however formally we may characterize subject-predicate grammars. "The way we talk" is mostly about the arguments of action—about actors, objects, instruments, loci, recipients, and so forth. It is drenched as well in the language of intention: it is difficult indeed to avoid animism in ordinary discourse. That is probably why so much social science discourse seems contrived and unnatural. The recent work of Roger Brown makes it plain, moreover, that our most innocent predicative utterances are shot through with implied intentionality and causation as far as ordinary listeners are concerned. Natural language, moreover, is also shot through with stance markers for indicating not only the stance of the speaker to the referent but to interlocutors: ways of stipulating what should be taken as given or presupposed, ways of indicating illocutionary intent by conventional linguistic means, ways of honoring the context for establishing occasion meaning in preference to timeless meaning. In folk societies, as Durojaya (1975) tells us, subtlety in this mode is taken as a mark of high intelligence and of sensitivity to the requirements of communal life.

The metaphoric mode seeks to establish vertical coherence by the selection of lexical elements to fit and to develop relations within a semantic domain, as with Keil's (1979) recent account of M-relations governed by class inclusion. Most of the concept attainment tasks that we set our subjects in developmental studies are based on metonymic rules, including most that I have used as well. As already noted, it favors context independence. It is the language of rationality when rationality is defined by reference to rules of logic and "right reasoning," whereas in the syntagmatic mode rationality is more likely to be defined by a person's ability to negotiate meaning socially.

In point of fact, the sort of intelligence required for getting on in the world is some interesting mix of the two governed by a supple plan for switching from the one to the other as appropriate—when to be sensitive to stance and presupposition, when to take context into account, when to let the story develop in its own lopsided way, and when as well to see the invariances and universalities and historical inevitabilities. As Katherine Nelson (in press) reminds us, the way in which we structure events and remember everyday happenings involves a mixture of the two.

I suspect that a good many developmental psychologists take it for granted (as indeed even Vygotsky did) that the "spontaneous" mode of narrative comes naturally and is inherent in the way we learn to *use* language (not acquire it, but use it). It is abstraction and metonymic order that must be inculcated—"scientific" concepts in Vygotsky's sense, that get one to the higher ground of abstraction. Yet there is something that makes me very suspicious of this point. The recent longitudinal study of the development of moral reasoning reported by Colby, Kohlberg, Gibbs, and Lieberman (1983) suggests that it takes many years, indeed a couple of decades, for human beings to get "naturally" to maturity in moral reasoning and that much of their difficulty is in recognizing the particularity of circumstances in the light of universal principles. We seem, by contrast, to develop sooner, more irreversibly, and more comprehensively with respect to reasoning about matters in the non-social world. There may even be a coarsening of human sympathy and sensitivity as the world becomes more technically and socially complex.

Perhaps we were well advised implicitly to place high value on young human beings growing up in a manner to deal with our increasingly technical society. But I have a parable to offer. About a decade ago, a high official of a famous institute of technology in a famous center of learning told me that it had been discovered that within 5 years of finishing, more than half of their graduates were principally involved in managing other human beings and what ought they to do about it?

What I should have told him is that if we thought they ought to be doing it well, we ought to devise a theory of development that could figure out the right way to assure that good result, managing to use in one sentence the three sacred words of ethical theory. Would I have been urging him to go into career management rather than working hard at a general developmental theory? Not on your life. My conviction, rather, is that there is no way of keeping a proper perspective within developmental theory without some sense of the alternative ways in which people are going to live out their careers and how we might conceivably arrange or rearrange the environment to make it easier for them to do so. But I am repeating myself. I have already said that I think developmental psychology is a policy science and, thereby, one of the sciences of the artificial. Without explicit value presuppositions, we will fall into the habit of forming implicit ones and lose such power as we might have either in furthering or opposing the values of the culture in which we find ourselves. Operating at our best and at our most fearless, we are a dangerous lot.

That danger does not come from our facts or from our hypotheses, but from how we relate them to the values to which the society adheres. Or to put it in a more philosophically up-market way: theories of development require a metatheory of values concerning the cultivation of the good man and the good society. They do not have to consult it every day of the week, nor should they set aside a pious Sunday for that pursuit alone. But if they fail to do it, fail to examine their value presupposition while hiding behind the naturalistic fallacy, developmental theory will risk serving as the mindless handmaiden of implicit beliefs in the culture rather than as a vigorous participant in the debate about the next generation.

Let me close with an unnerving quotation from Martin Joos's (1964) book, *The English Verb,* one that may keep these deep matters we are discussing from becoming frozen: "Within the modal system, English does not distinguish between duty and logic. And if not there, English can't do it anywhere within the whole grammatical system." To be consistent, then, I cannot tell you clearly whenever you *ought* to be convinced by the *logic* of my case or whether it is your *duty* to be so!

REFERENCES

Austin, J. (1962). *How to do things with words*. Oxford: Oxford University Press.

Berger, P., & Luckmann, T. (1966). *The social construction of reality*. New York: Doubleday.

Bruner, J. S. (1980). *Under five in Britain*. London: Grant MacIntryre.

Colby, A., Kohlberg, L., Gibbs, J., & Lieberman, M. (1983). A longitudinal study of moral judgement. *Monographs of the Society for Research in Child Development, 48* (1–2, Serial No. 200).

Drucker, P. (1955). *The practice of management*, London: Heinemann.

Durkheim, E. (1965). *The elementary forms of religious life*. New York: Free Press.

Durojaya, M. (1975). *Cross cultural interpretation of intelligence*. Paper presented at a Symposium, Cross Cultural Perception in Cognition, International Congress of Psychology, Paris.

Feldman, C. (1974). Pragmatic features of natural language. In M. W. LaGally, R. A. Fox, & A. Bruck (Eds.), *Papers from the Tenth Regional Meeting, Chicago Linguistic Society*, Chicago: Chicago Linguistic Society. (pp. 151–160).

Geertz, C. (1973). *The interpretation cultures: selected essays*. New York: Basic Books.

Heider, F. (1958). *The psychology of interpersonal relations*. New York: Wiley.

Jakobson, R. (1960). Linguistics and poetics. In T. A. Sebeok (Ed.), *Style in language*. Cambridge, MA.: MIT Press.

Joss, M. (1964). *The English verb: Form and meaning* (2nd ed.). Madison: University of Wisconsin Press.

Keil, F. C. (1979). *Semantic and conceptual development*. Cambridge, MA: Harvard University Press.

Kelly, G. (1955). *The psychology of personal constructs*. New York: Norton.

Kessen, W. (1979). The American child and other cultural inventions. *American Psychologist, 34*, 815–820.

Nelson, K. (in press). The syntagmatics and paradigmatics of conceptual development. In S. Kuczaj (Ed.), *Language, cognition & culture*. Hillsdale, NJ: Lawrence Erlbaum Associates.

Paley, V. (1981). *Wally's stories*. Cambridge, MA: Harvard University.

Piaget, J. (1952). *The origins of intelligence in children*. New York: International Universities Press.

Simon, H. (1957). *Models of man*. New York: Wiley.

Sperber, D. (1973). *Rethinking symbolism*. Cambridge: Cambridge University Press.

Werner, H. (1948). *Comparative psychology of mental development*. New York: Follett.

Wertheimer, R. (1972). *Significance of sense: Meaning, modality & morality*. Ithaca: Cornell University Press.

White, S. (1976). *Human development in today's world*. New York: Little, Brown.

DISCUSSION

KAGAN: Let me just raise one issue that pertains to the statement you made about normal development. If you meant that development only occurs in an environment, then of course you are right. There is no "normal" development. But once I stipulate an environment, let us say one of objects and people (that's an austere environment), then there is a development, without an ought. So, what did you intend: that one cannot say anything about a normal change sequence given an environment or not? One example is acid rain. Suppose biologists find that everyone starts to develop six fingers because the pH of the water has changed. Now normal development will consist of six-fingered hands, given that environment.

BRUNER: Well, to start off with, I want to talk about the environment over which we have control, although we do have some control over acid rain, and undoubtedly there will be some effects of having six fingers. Indeed, I do mean that in any given environment there is something that can be called a set of normal reactions. We don't have to accept the notion that there is a single one.

Then I want to come back to something that I can't say strongly enough. Personality theory always put me off a little because personality theory has people who are not in places. When I think about a person who is nowhere and you tell me about his dispositional properties and that he has certain kinds of ego defenses that operate or he has a self-construct of a certain type, I know two points that I would want to make. First, Roger Barker used to say that if you want to account for human behavior, find out where the person is. In the post office they behaved post office, and in the schoolrooms they behaved schoolroom, and so forth. Second, I like the implicit theories of personality that I get from some of my novelist heroes; for example, imagine Joyce's Stephen Daedelus living anywhere but in Dublin. He talks about walking the streets in Dublin in search of the epiphanies of the ordinary. What he means is that he is relating himself to aspects of the environment that are familiar, that are made for Dubliners and by Dubliners. Now *that* I also want to include in the description of the environment. The external notion that there is an environment that somehow is forevermore and has been there from the start and somehow is geological—I don't believe it. To come back to M. Foucault's crazy, marvelous little book, *The Archeology of Knowledge* (it's just a small book and it will keep you disturbed for at least a week), the point I want to make is that in the sector of this environment that one lives one is influenced by the reality that has been created, and you cannot talk about response just in terms of some external description of the environment. There has to be an internal one.

I'm going to hawk another book, a magnificent book written by a young anthropologist who, alas, died in an accident when she went back to visit the Ilonget people in the Philippines whom she was studying, Michelle Rosaldo. She published one book before she died called *Knowledge and Passion,* in which she talks about the internal reality, internal to the culture, but which nonetheless has public meaning. These are part of what I mean when I talk about the fact that you cannot tell me about what the normal responses are until you really give me a description of it to the participants and how they negotiate its various meanings. So, it's not just in a trivial sense that I mean that behavior is a function of person and environment. Environment turns out to be a much more complicated concept than that.

KAPLAN: Jerry, it has something to do with what psychologists do often; that is, treat acts as if they don't have objects and treat thought as though there is a knowing, without raising the question about the status of the object. Now, how do you deal with the status of the objects? Do you treat them as internal to mental activity? We usually take the environment as defined by specialized experts. But we also deal with what Kenneth Burke calls "the scene," and the scene is always intrinsically linked to the agent.

BRUNER: I think the brief answer to that, Bernie, is that that's initially what forced me into being a constructivist about reality and about psychology. I just cannot believe that there is a reality that impinges on us. I can't help but tell you a story. There was a student of Mason Haire's when Mason was teaching at MIT who turned out to be a brilliant young physicist who came to his opening two or three lectures in psychology at MIT and then stopped showing up. Around the middle of the term, Mason ran into him as he was walking around the campus at MIT and said, "There's nothing personal about this, but I really am quite interested because I understand that you are a very bright physicist. Why did you stop coming to class?" And this diffident young man said, "Well, all right, I'll tell you. If the only thing that you can say about the world is that it is an *S,* a stimulus, then you can't be a very interesting field." That's basically *the* point.

BERNSTEIN: I would like to ask about something that was unsaid to see if we can get it clear. You began by emphasizing the stringency and your suspicions of those who want to draw the holy trinity out of the facts. On the other hand, you stated that you cannot be a developmental psychologist without taking a value position. What you did after that is to give a critique of certain value positions—a very interesting critique of why a certain aspect of developmental psychology has become dominant. What is unclear, however, to me is the sense in which you do think a value presupposition, if made explicit, can be defended, warranted, justified. In a way that's what you were doing. You were giving arguments for it but there is, you might say, a deep text, or substratum of the epistemological position that would say, particularly in using the language of axiology, "Well, that only goes back to another set of value presuppositions." I want to find out if you are Weberian or not on this particular position.

BRUNER: I put it this way. First of all, I do take stands and they are stands that are very akin to the ones that you ended up with. That is to say, I think we're a dangerous lot and may have to take hemlock one day because what we do is to raise what for the establishment is the spectre of pluralism, and I want to call it a spectre—that this is not the natural or only way to do it. What we do is to raise consciousness in a fashion akin to the way in which the new version of the women's movement started off in the 1960s to raise consciousness about the question of how you should define woman and the potentialities that she has for entry within the society. And here we're doing it in a somewhat different way.

I take stands that come out of a set of axioms about man that I cannot give you an existential justification of in terms of factual statement. I keep, as a kind of meta-ethical theory, the view that many is better than one. I can find no way in which I can justify the notion that many alternatives set before people is better than one alternative, and I know that this is the thing that has always locked me in political controversy, and I mean to go on behaving in this unseemly way, yet I can't justify it. So, am I in a Weberian position? I think, "Yes." The fact of the matter is that Weber really was a much more politicized theorist than you made it plain that he was. For example, one of the things that Weber did was to point out the extent to which the very bureaucratization of the society digs in those illusions in such a way as to obscure their origins. In a sense, what he did was to give fuel to those who began to represent the opposition to the over-governed state, the bureau-cratized state, without taking a stand that the whole should be wiped out—a very seemly stance for an intellectual. Perhaps it's a little bit too much lost in thought; nevertheless it is very consistent with the role of being an intellec-tual. That's the only basis I have for justifying—that it somehow fits into the temperament that does the other things that I do as well—which is no justifi-cation at all but a description of me.

GILLIGAN: I want to follow the same queston but raise the ante a little bit. Pluralism is a very appealing solution to the whole question of value presupposition.

BRUNER: It isn't really a solution. I know that.

GILLIGAN: However, in the center of that solution as a developmental psychol-ogist you suggested a moment of choice or trade-off. You asked if anybody had done a study that shows the growth of formal thinking may lead to a decline in the capacity for other forms of thinking—more metaphoric, and so forth. I want to tell you an observation made on data that had to do with adolescents who were at exactly that point in development, eighth graders, from a thesis of a student at Harvard, Betty Bardige, who looked at the kids' journals and their responses to films that were shown in a social studies class on *Facing History and Ourselves.* The concrete operational children took the story literally—the film of the Warsaw ghetto, the Milgram experiment, and so forth—and had responses to it such as, "It is so sad. Why doesn't someone stop them?" As the children gained the capacity to take into account point of view, multiple explanations, the construction of the story, [then] the power of the narrative, the literal narrative, was subject to all of that secondary reflection and there was diminution or falling off of evidence of the capacity for that kind of direct, emotional if you wish, response to the story. Let's assume for the moment that at that moment in development there really is a trade-off in that the fostering of the one kind of thought you described is at the expense of the other. Knowing that as a developmental psychologist, what position do you want to take?

BRUNER: I have no hesitation whatsoever in the position that I take. I am willing to risk the stability of the society to make it possible for the choice to be battled out, to be negotiated, because I really think that education is culture-creating and not culture-transmitting. However, if you ask me whether that derives from my being a developmental psychologist as compared to what I'll call for a moment a moralist I will have to say it comes from my position as a moralist, not as a developmental psychologist.

KAPLAN: Does your position as a moralist enter into what constitutes for you developmental psychology, or do you split them?

BRUNER: I certainly do not split them, as you know. What I do is research which I think can somehow make clear the alternative ways in which growth can proceed in different kinds of environments. Now if somebody says that that's tendentious, yes, it is. It's perfectly clear that when the then Governor of California (now our President) decided to ban a course of study, for example, which a group of us had put together to show the different value positions that people can take and still maintain a kind of intrinsic dignity, the notion that I had cannot be derived anymore from *my* science than Ronald Reagan was able to derive his position from *his* science. However, I can do one thing which makes me more dangerous than him. I can give people a much more interesting menu of possibilities than he can, and that makes me political as well as a scientist.

BERNSTEIN: This last response is interesting because what you do belies what you say. What you are attempting to do all the time without claiming deductive proof is to give an argument, is to show why certain things are wrong or deficient. It seems to me there is then an implicit appeal that while it's not deductive and there are alternatives, it's a better argument than the alternatives. In that sense, you are appealing to some structure of rationality or argumentation which is not to be assimilated; "Well, this is just my arbitrary axiological bias and here I stand. I can say nothing else." That's not what you do. You are always arguing, and I think it's important to make that clear.

BRUNER: Not only am I arguing but I am also doing t tests. I never thought that I would get into a discussion about the value of t tests.

BERNSTEIN: I didn't ask that question. [Laughter]

BRUNER: But it seems to me that the nature of the argument is that there are assertions that I can make about what very, very likely will follow as consequences to doing certain kinds of things which offer what I called a moment ago, in the style of computer sciences, "a menu of alternatives." In doing so, it seems to me that my argumentation is tremendously buttressed by that apparatus of proof. Now, it is possible for somebody to say, "I think only with my gun and my blood," you know, and we have had it in our own lifetime. "To hell with your t tests, Bruner. We know better and, as a matter of fact, to be sure that you won't do any more t tests, we have a place where we can put you." And, they put a lot of people there. So that I realize that the very apparatus of argumentation, both derivations from axiological positions as well as proof of empirical propositions, that those also are matters that society adjudicates in some way as to whether or not they want to use those as a basis for proceeding. That's why we are both dangerous and beleaguered.

WARTOFSKY: I won't be quite as cruel as Dick here. I won't claim that you are saying one thing and doing another, but I do think there is something I could possibly formulate as "Bruner's paradox." First, you said (and I agree) that any developmental theory entails a value position. The second point was that taking such a value position guides or orients one's research. Then you said research can't tell you what you desire. But if your value position is going to orient your research, then it would seem to me your research is going to tell you *only* what you desire if it's oriented by that value position.

BRUNER: That is not only Bruner's paradox, but that is the paradox of all of the social sciences.

WARTOFSKY: Okay. The second point has to do with the reflective-impulsive stuff which disturbs me. I mean, if I can be a manic-depressive or a social-democrat, I can certainly be an impulsive-reflective. [Laughter] And the idea that children lose their metaphorical, narrative, or creative understanding when they are forced or trained to become reflective seems to me to be wrong. Now what may heppen is that, as we often do, we may de-train in one respect while we train in the other by separating these two features in the way schools ordinarily do. As we know, art and subjects of that sort, and playtime, are outside the curriculum; in the deathless words of the Board of Education of the City of New York when I was in high school, "Art is a useless frill." (They were attempting at that time to close down the High School of Music and Art that I was then attending.) In a sense, there is a separation between the reflective and the impulsive, but I am a little disturbed by the characterization of Vonnegut or of Robert Lowell as impulsive types—as against what else? Certainly Lowell is one of the most reflectively deliberate craftsmen working in a metonymic mode and the construction of a highly crafted work of art. So the impulsiveness has to, in a sense, be strained through, directed, or given a disciplined form—what Friedrich Schiller called "shaped feeling," in his *Letters on Aesthetic Education*. It has to be given a reflective character in order for it to come out as art. I didn't like the sort of trade-off between the two in which development seems to go either one way or the other, as if it wasn't precisely the interaction between the two which is what we want.

BRUNER: I think we're in complete agreement. What happens in the cultivation of these matters is that one is presented as favorable; the other has to go underground as a sin. You are talking about Robert Lowell who, as you know, was a close friend of mine. One of the great events that happened in his life is when one of his early teachers, John Crowe Ransom, said to him, "Listen, you can be both angry and think."

KAGAN: This is quite a shift and it returns us to your answer to my question, Jerry, which I was not happy with. You said something that I think all of us agree with—if one takes a subjective frame, then why care about the objective environment. It seems to me that a dangerous thing is happening in modern social science: it's a confusion between a subjective and an objective epistemology. Do we care about the experiences of von Frisch's bees? Von Frisch noted some lawful relations between objective aspects of the environment and objective aspects of the motions of bees and he generated elegant, objective propositions which satisfy us and provide a sense of the aesthetic. If bees could talk and said to him, "Sir, that's really not our experience," no one would claim the original descriptions were wrong. Subjective experience and phenomenal report are important for my personal interpretation of my life and action. But, the objective description need not accommodate to it. Tex Garner has a lovely sentence. He says that we know that perception is holistic, unitary, and immediate; but psychologists violate the unity with analysis and generate elegant, objective descriptions.

BRUNER: I think it's perfectly clear that Jerry and I are going to come to blows before this meeting is over. If *he* thinks that *I* mean—I can say this to Jerry because we've been old friends for years—that I mean that the constructed world, this world culture in which one lives, the internal way of defining the nature of the world, has to do with asking somebody how their perception works, he surely hasn't fully understood what I said. What I am talking about you can't get from bees. Bees, curiously enough, interest me only slightly. What I am interested in is that the thing typical of our species is that we took a leap such that we live in a stipulative world. Bees don't promise each other, for example, nor do they have jails for those who break promises, or lawsuits that you can bring against them. There is a range of behavior which, if you understand it from top down, leaves me deeply unimpressed by the immediate applicability of statements of the von Frisch type to human beings.

The part I am interested in is the fact that the formation of the stipulative world, the way in which we respond to symbol systems and the expectancies that get built by technology, is constrained by our biological nature. I have never believed that culture can be regarded as completely independent of our biological nature. Culture is a biological product, a point which you too have made. Look, I proposed a theory of perception based on the notion of successive bursts of hypothesis testing which couldn't be further away from phenomenology. That has nothing at all to do with the structure of phenomenology. The next question is why experience seems seamless while the underlying processes are not seamless but a series of almost saccadic processes. That itself is an interesting question which Tex overlooked.

KAGAN: But let's go back to your statement that there is no such thing as normal development.

BRUNER: I didn't say that.

KAGAN: Can you elaborate your statement that it doesn't make much sense to talk about normal development?

BRUNER: Well, let me give it to you in terms of an example which is almost emblematic, a study of Mike Coles with one of his graduate students. They did a study on tutoring in which they would reward and correct for deviation. He happened to have two kinds of subjects, one of them black, middle-class kids and the other black from a working-class background. The kids from a working-class background showed a steady decline in performance; the ones who came from a middle-class background showed a steady increment in performance. They were defining the situation differently. The kids who declined said, ''I can't get that guy off my back,'' and the other group said, ''Boy, he was really helpful.'' So, what am I going to do with the theory of reinforcement which is based on how reinforcement comes through the filter of the cultural circumstances?

There is one other thing too about the ''objective'' world. It has crucial indications that I think operate as determinants, complex symbolic indicators like gross national product or rates of mobility or money supply. There are many steps between individual behavior and things like gross national product. And obviously the economic state of things has a very powerful effect on the range of alternatives. But that is not the point entirely. The point is that once GNP becomes an indicator, a culturally acceptable symbol, it begins to produce behavior relevant to it. So that one is not only responding to "external" economic conditions, but to the symbolic rendering that we give them in regular discourse. So that economics *in fact* limits options for action, and symbolically alters our response to those options. That is the typical case.

3

Remapping Development: The Power of Divergent Data

Carol Gilligan
Harvard University

The search for a moral beacon to illuminate the path of human life is an eternal quest. The wish for a right answer to the ultimate questions of how to live and what to do arises again in each generation, drawing sustenance in the Western tradition from Plato's claim that virtue is one as well as from the Biblical injunction of only one God. But with the assumption of this quest in a secular age by psychologists of human development and the transposition of its unitary vision into a great chain of stages in invariant sequence, the question arises of in whose terms or from what perspective these claims are being made? Who frames the values presupposed in theories of human development? Who defines the ideal of maturity that welds judgments of progress to observations of change?

I begin by noting the human construction of theories of human development not to arrive at the familiar debate between moral monotheism and value relativism or moral nihilism but to lay the groundwork for an alternative formulation. By asking the psychologist's question of how we come to hold moral values and tracing the ontogenesis of values to the experience of human relationships, I will claim that two moral predispositions inhere in the structure of human connection, given the inequality and the attachment or interdependence of child and parent. Thus in contrast to unitary theories of moral growth or the counterposition of an endless variation, I will distinguish two moral orientations that evolve through different dimensions of relationships and identify these two dimensions of relationship as the coordinates for a new map of development. This remapping reveals the perspective toward relationships embedded in current stage theories by expanding the angle of vision. But it also explains why the adoption of a single perspective creates a persistent problem of discrepant data.

My approach in this paper is historical in retracing a process of discovery that began with the observation of a discrepancy between theory and data in the field of moral judgment research. As the project extended through a series of studies conducted over a period of 10 years, the observation of discrepancy led to its exploration and to the consideration of its implications for the psychology of human development. In demonstrating the power of divergent data to illuminate current theories and inform new models of growth, I hope to identify the value presuppositions that have colored our developmental theories and to explain how different value positions reflect different ways of experiencing and understanding relationships (Gilligan, 1982; Gilligan, Langdale, Lyons, & Murphy, 1982).

THE OBSERVATION OF DISCREPANCY

In the early 1970s I began to study the relationship between moral judgment and action and the role of experience in moral development. I was interested at the time in discovering how people thought about actual rather than hypothetical moral conflicts and in how their thinking affected their actions and how their actions affected their conceptions of morality and of themselves. The awareness of a discrepancy between theory and data grew out of an observation made in the course of selecting a sample for a longitudinal study of moral and ego development. The sample was to be randomly chosen from a list of college seniors who as sophomores had taken a course with Lawrence Kohlberg on moral and political choice. Reviewing the list, I noticed that of the 70 students who enrolled, 20 subsequently dropped the course. This fact, although not remarkable in itself, was striking to me because of the 20 students, 16 were women and only 10 women remained in the class. When the women who left were contacted and interviewed, their responses to questions about moral conflict were at first hard to understand. Their descriptions of moral problems they faced did not fit the prevailing categories of moral thought but seemed rather to confirm the opinion that women confuse moral problems with problems of interpersonal relationships.

The recurrence of this observation of difference between women's moral thinking and theories of moral development was prepared although not intended by the decision to base a study of judgment and action on a sample of pregnant women who were considering abortion. The study was designed to discover how the women thought about this decision, whether they construed it in moral terms and if so, what was the nature of that construction. Because females had been excluded from the research samples upon which both Piaget and Kohlberg had based their descriptions of moral judgment, the abortion decision study was the first to draw moral categories from the analysis of women's langauge and thought. This analysis revealed a reiterative use of the words "selfish" and "responsible" to define the moral parameters of choice, and this language called attention to a construction of the moral problem as a problem of responsibility in relationships. In this relational construction, responsibility connoted not an obligation to fulfill an abstract duty but an injunction to respond with care and to avoid hurt. The word selfish conversely denoted a morally problematic separation of others from self.

The abortion dilemma, thus construed, was a dilemma of relationships, premised on the recognition of self and other as connected and therefore interdependent. This premise conflicts with the view of self and other as separate that underlies the understanding of moral problems as problems of conflicting rights. Assuming relationship, the women identified the moral problem as a problem of care. Seeing no way not to act and no way of acting that would not affect the connection between others and self, they asked whether it was responsible or irresponsible, moral or immoral, to have a child or to end a pregnancy in circumstances where caring for the child was for various reasons problematic. Consequently, the question was not whether to act or whether action could be justified but rather how to act responsibly in a situation where hurt seemed inescapable. Rather than appealing primarily to principles of fairness and rights, the women centered their consideration on their understanding of responsibility and care and their knowledge of human relationships.

This formulation of morality as a problem of care and responsibility in relationships, premised on an assumption of connection and associated with a view of self and other as interdependent, challenged the opposition between self and other and thus the distinction between egoism and altruism that traditionally has been central to the construction of the moral domain. The abortion dilemma, by highlighting the fact of connection, illuminated the assumption of inter-dependence that previously had rendered the moral judgments of women opaque. Seen in this light, the focus on relationships in women's moral thinking, rather than signaling a failure to differentiate the moral from the interpersonal domain, signified a different conception of morality that was bound to a different understanding of relationships and a different way of thinking about the self as a moral agent.

Key to this work was a shift in methodology that removed definitional categories from the instruments of measurement. By asking people to describe moral conflicts in their lives and to discuss choices they faced rather than presenting them with dilemmas for resolution, it was possible to identify ways of constructing moral problems that differed from those represented in the prevailing instruments of psychological assessment. Because women's thinking had not been considered in defining the moral domain, theirs was a different voice. Although this difference had repeatedly been noted in the psychological literature on moral development and was cited by Piaget as the reason for excluding girls from his initial study of children's games, it had previously been interpreted as indicative of a problem in women's development, variously explained but seen as having no theoretical significance. Yet the analysis of the differences observed in girls' and women's moral thinking pointed instead to a problem in theory—a failure to imagine or represent a different conception of morality and self.

The values of justice and autonomy that are presupposed in current theories of human growth and embedded in the definitions of morality and of the self imply a view of the individual as separate and of relationships as either heirarchical or contractual, bound by the alternatives of constraint and cooperation. In contrast, the values of care and connection that emerge saliently in women's thinking imply a view of self and other as interdependent and of relationships as networks sustained by activities of care-giving and response. The two moral voices that articulate these visions thus denote different ways of viewing the world. Within each perspective, all the key terms of social understanding take on different meanings, reflecting a change in the imagery of relationships and signifying a shift in orientation. Like the shifting perception of the vase and the faces in the illustration of the ambiguous figure, there appear to be two ways of perceiving self in relation to others, both grounded in reality but imposing on that reality a different organization. Because moral judgments, as Piaget noted, reflect the logic of social understanding, these different forms of organization emerge most clearly as different ways of defining and resolving moral problems.

The nature of these differences and their implications are clarified by the example of two 4-year-old children who were playing together and wanted to play different games (Gilligan, in press). In this particular version of this common dilemma, the girl said, "Let's play next-door neighbors." "I want to play pirates," the boy replied. "Okay," said the girl, "then you can be the pirate who lives next door." By comparing this inclusive solution of combining the games with the fair solution of taking turns and playing each game for an equal period, it is possible to see not only how these two approaches yield different ways of solving a problem in relationships but also how each solution differentially affects the identity of the games and the experience of the relationship.

The fair solution of taking turns leaves the identity of each game intact, providing an opportunity for each child to experience the other's imaginative world and regulating the exchange by the imposition of a rule based on a premise of equal respect. The inclusive solution, in contrast, transforms both games through their combination: The neighbor game is changed by the presence of a pirate living next door; the pirate game is changed by bringing the pirate into a neighborhood. As each child thus enters the world of the other's imagination, that world is visibly transformed by his or her presence. The identity of each separate game yields to a new creation as the relationship between the children gives rise to a game that neither had separately imagined. Although the fair solution protects identity and ensures equality within the context of a relationship, the inclusive solution transforms identity through the experience of relationship. The elaboration of these different views of self in relationship and the exploration of their significance for moral understanding and self-definition became the agenda for the research project in its second phase.

THE EXPLORATION OF DIVERGENT DATA

"If we hope to live not just for moment to moment, but in true consciousness of our existence, then our greatest need and most difficult achievement is to find meaning in our lives" (p. 3). Thus Bruno Bettelheim (1977) in defining the goal of development also states the problem faced by theorists of development, the imposition of meaning on change. That judgments of progress, stasis, and regression are made on the basis of value premises and from a perspective seems increasingly clear. But the extent to which a particular set of value premises and a particular perspective have governed only only the understanding of development but also the instruments for its measurement has not been equally apparent. The discordance heard between women's voices and theories of human development opened an avenue of exploration by revealing different conceptions of morality and self that were tied to different ways of perceiving relationships. The implications of these two perspectives for understanding both male and female development and for thinking about instruments of assessment pointed to the need for an enlarged developmental conception and new methods of analysis that could encompass and directly represent what previously appeared as anomalous data.

The systematic investigation of the two moral orientations began with a study designed in conjunction with Michael Murphy to isolate the variables of gender, age, and type of dilemma that previously had been confounded in moral judgment research. The study hinged on the creation of reliable procedures for distinguishing the two moral orientations and the two modes of self-description in open-ended interview data. Nona Lyons (1980, 1982, 1983) demonstrated that it was possible reliably to distinguish considerations of justice and care in people's description of "real-life" moral dilemmas, and Sharry Langdale (1983) demonstrated that Lyons' coding procedure could be used in analyzing responses to hypothetical moral dilemmas. In addition, Lyons constructed a manual for coding responses to an open-ended question about self-description by identifying a relational component that appeared in most people's self-descriptions and differentiating between two conceptions of self in relation to others—as "separate/objective" and as "connected."

The data used in these analyses were drawn from a sample of 144 males and females matched for high levels of intelligence, education and occupation at nine ages ranging across the life cycle from 6 to 60. Working with the data from an intensively interviewed subsample of 36 males and females (2 males and 2 females at each of the nine ages), Lyons found that most people used considerations of both justice and care in constructing and resolving moral problems and in evaluating the choices they made. However, one orientation generally was used with greater frequency, reflected by the number of considerations presented within that mode. This difference observed in the frequency of considerations of justice and care led to the scoring of predominant moral orientation, and a parallel phenomenon of differential frequency was observed and used in scoring predominant mode of self-description.

These findings, reported by Lyons, revealed that considerations of justice and care could be distinguished in the ways people framed and resolved moral problems and in their evaluation of the choices they made; that these two modes of moral reasoning were associated with different ways of describing the self in relation to others—with justice related to the depiction of self as separate in relation to others and care to the description of self as connected to others; that major and minor modes of moral reasoning and self-description could be identified in most people's thinking; and finally, that the use of these modes and their salience in people's thinking although not gender specific were gender related. Although no individual was confined to any particular mode by virtue of gender and most people in fact used both modes, the women in this sample tended to rely more on considerations of care and response in defining and resolving moral problems and to describe themselves in the connected mode. The men, as a group, relied more on considerations of justice and rights and tended to define themselves as separate in relation to others.

The discovery that the voice that speaks of connection, not hurting, care, and response could reliably be differentiated from the voice that speaks of equality, reciprocity, justice, and rights and the finding that these different modes of moral discourse appeared in conjunction with different forms of self-description pointed to the common grounding of these distinctions in two perspectives toward relationships (see Gilligan, 1984). These perspectives were clarified by the discovery that the two modes of moral discourse shared a common moral vocabulary, but that within each mode the meaning of individual words changed. This discovery then led to the recognition that these differences in meaning arose from an underlying shift in the perspective toward others and that these shifts in perspective denoted two ways of understanding relationships. Distinguishing the moralities of justice and care by delineating the different understanding of relationships embedded in each, Lyons defined the two perspectives toward others as the perspectives of reciprocity and response—one rooted in impartiality and the search for objectivity, the capacity to distance oneself and determine fair rules for mediating relationships; one grounded in the specific contexts of others, the capacity to perceive people in their own terms and to respond to their needs.

For centuries these two lines of morality have wandered through the Western tradition, appearing in the contrasts between reason and compassion, fairness and forgiveness, justice and mercy, and emerging repeatedly although by no means exclusively in contrasts between women and men. These distinctions implied an underlying division between thought and feeling, a separation between the process of judgment and the capacity for response. But the association with gender focuses the problem in this formulation because the implication that women are thoughtless and men without feeling clearly can not be sustained. Instead there appear to be two modes of thinking that carry different implications of feeling and signify different ways of perceiving others and knowing oneself. Attention to women's thinking thus broadens the definition of self and the categories of moral thought, and this expanded conceptual framework provides a new way of listening to differences not only between but also within the thinking of women and men.

Such an extension in the conception of the moral domain has been advocated in philosophy by Lawrence Blum (1980) who challenges the dominant Kantian position to argue that altruistic concerns and sympathetic emotions can be considered morally good. This view is supported as well in psychology by Martin Hoffman (1976) who, in turning to the study of empathy and altruism, points out that "Western psychology has evolved along lines seemingly antithetical to giving consideration for others a central place in the overall view of personality" (p. 124). Hoffman criticizes "the doctrinaire view . . . that altruistic behavior can always be explained in terms of instrumental, self-serving motives in the actor" (p. 124)—the view, in short, that people are selfish and altruism always a guise. But the current inquiry, sympathetic to these efforts and indebted to their clarification, begins with the awareness of two different perspectives toward relationships. It also asks whether the distinction between egoism and altruism and the sharp division between rationality and emotion, which have informed the discussion not only of morality but also of love in the Western world, are not themselves embedded in a particular perspective toward relationships, one premised on a fundamental separation between other and self.

The existence of two moral perspectives and the way in which a unitary vision blurs their representation were clarified by the work of Langdale, who analyzed the moral judgments made by the entire sample of 144 males and females, of which the intensively interviewed group was a part. All participants in the study were asked to resolve two hypothetical dilemmas, the Heinz dilemma constructed by Kohlberg as a dilemma of conflicting rights and the Kathy or the Sara dilemma, two versions of a problem presented by women in the abortion decision study and constructed as a dilemma of conflicting responsibilities and relationships. The aim of the study was to investigate the interaction between the variables of age, gender, and type of dilemma and the presence and predominance of the two moral orientations. The "real-life" dilemmas that were generated by the members of the intensively interviewed subsample provided a measure of spontaneous moral orientation that made it possible to ascertain how the framing of standardized dilemmas affected the two moral orientations.

Using Lyons' coding procedures for distinguishing considerations of justice and care, Langdale found that in each dilemma (Heinz, Kathy and Sara), both orientations appeared and could be reliably coded; that the use of these orientations was significantly associated with gender across all the dilemmas, with care more predominant in the thinking of the females and justice in the thinking of the males; and that the two moral orientations appeared systematically across the life cycle with no significant differences in age. In addition to these overall findings of orientation distinction and gender differences, Langdale observed a variation in the frequency of the orientations across different dilemmas, with the Heinz dilemma eliciting the highest percentage of justice considerations in females and the Real-Life and the Sara dilemmas the highest percentage of considerations of care among males (see also D. K. Johnston, 1985).

Because the representation of the two moral orientations in reasoning about the Heinz dilemma significantly differ for both sexes from their representation in the Real-Life dilemma, the Heinz dilemma, although the most frequently used dilemma in moral development research, does not appear to provide an accurate reflection of the way people think about moral problems in their lives. For females, this dispartiy was far greater, given the predominance of care in their spontaneous moral orientation. Although the pull toward justice reasoning in the Heinz dilemma seems to confirm an equation of moral judgment with justice reasoning, the responses of females renders that equation somewhat problematic as illustrated by the history of Kohlberg's (1969, 1981, 1984) research. The problem revealed by the responses of females draws attention to the problem in this representation of male moral reasoning, given the presence of considerations of care in men's thinking about real moral dilemmas.

The unexpected finding of a difference between the appearance of the two moral orientations in the two versions of the abortion dilemma further elucidates this problem by revealing how the question posed by the investigator influences the judgments made. Although the issue of abortion remained constant in the dilemmas of Kathy and Sara, and the story itself, although differently told, remained essentially the same, the question asked in each version was changed. The open-ended question of the Sara dilemma ("What should Sara do?") elicited considerations of justice and care that were not significantly different from those represented on the Real-Life dilemma. In contrast, the Kathy dilemma posed a question that was analogous in the Heinz dilemma, by specifying a given resolution and inquiring about its justification ("Should Kathy have an abortion?"). Like the Heinz dilemma, although to a lesser extent, the responses to the Kathy dilemma when compared with the measure of spontaneous moral orientation showed an increase in justice considerations, which were joined by women to considerations of care and associated in men's thinking with a decrease in care considerations. Thus the two moral orientations were sensitive to variations in the question, which affected the presence of care and justice reasoning for each sex in somewhat different ways. These effects, however, did not override the association of these orientations with gender.

The findings of gender difference in this sample were of particular interest because the sample had been selected to test Kohlberg's claim that gender differences in moral reasoning can be accounted for by differences in education and occupation. Yet in this sample where males and females were matched for high levels of intelligence, education, and professional status, gender differences in moral orientation remained. In interpreting these findings, it is essential to distinguish between Lyons' scoring of moral orientation and Kohlberg's scoring of moral stage. In support of Kohlberg's claim, there were no significant differences found in this sample between mean Kohlberg stage scores for males and females. There were, however, highly significant gender differences found in moral orientation. These differences in moral orientation appeared on the Heinz as well as the other dilemmas.

The confusion between stage and orientation thus seemed to run deeper in Kohlberg's framework, complicating the discussion of gender differences but also revealing the problem in a unitary formulation of moral development. Langdale, in untangling this confusion, found that individuals, primarily females (86% females, 14% males), with care represented in their predominant moral orientation have significantly lower Kohlberg stage scores than individuals, primarily males (69% males, 31% females), with care unrepresented in their predominant moral orientation (i.e., predominant care or split orientation vs. predominant justice orientation). The finding of significant gender differences in the use of each orientation together with the finding that the predominant representation of care is associated with significantly lower scores on Kohlberg's scale of moral development suggests that gender differences reported on Kohlberg's measure derive not from the fact of gender per se but rather from the greater tendency of females to frame and resolve moral problems in the care orientation. The primary use of the care orientation thus creates a liability within Kohlberg's framework, lowering moral judgment scores by an average of 50 points. This finding in turn reflects the fact that Kohlberg conceived moral development within the single perspective of the justice orientation.

The consequences of this conception for the assessment of moral development in both sexes are illustrated by the moral judgments at age 15 of two children, Amy and Jake, whose judgments at 11 elucidated the divergence between the justice and care orientations. At 11, when Amy was asked whether Heinz should steal the drug, she replied that he shouldn't steal but his wife shouldn't die either. Transforming the question from whether stealing could be justified to how Heinz could best care for his wife in this situation, she saw the moral problem arising not from a conflict of rights but from the druggist's failure of response. Her low score on Kohlberg's scale reflected this formulation, since her shift in the focus of the dilemma from the relationship of law and life to the relationships between the druggist, Heinz, and his wife turned her attention away from considerations of justice and rights and to considerations of care and response, which guided her strategy for resolving the problem.

At 15, Amy clearly understands the logic of both orientations and reflects their tension as she vacillates between them in judging Heinz's dilemma. Commenting that she "hated these dilemmas as much last time as I do now," she begins by questioning whether stealing was the best response in this situation. Thus when asked whether Heinz should steal the drug, she says, "I said the same thing (last time) if I remember what I said, which is that I really don't know." Yet then she switches direction, saying, "I mean, yes, I think he should steal the drug." Believing that another way besides stealing could be found for obtaining the drug or the money and yet noting the number of people in the world who are dying and starving, she finds no easy answer to the problem posed. The dilemma seems to her at once logically soluble and essentially implausible. Clearly life comes before profit in a hierarchy of values ("I think human life is a little more important than the man's profit") but it remains unclear that stealing would solve either the more general problem of distribution or the particular problem of Heinz and his wife in this situation. Everything she knows about cancer suggests that it cannot be cured by a single treatment and that a drug for curing cancer would not be "sitting out on the shelf of the drugstore." If these events took place in a small town, as the narrative of the dilemma describes, then if the drug disappeared, Heinz would immediately be suspected. Imagining Heinz in jail having saved his wife and deciding "it (was) worth it," she also imagines the wife alone, in need of money and additional treatment.

Returning to the question of stealing, she wonders about the druggist's perspective: "Maybe (his) property is important for some reason; there could be another side to the druggist's story." In the end, she concludes that it is not "as much a question of right and wrong as just what you feel, which is more important. It's a question of importance, not a truth." Her difficulty in seeing a unitary truth that would guide the resolution of this dilemma signifies the tension in her thinking between two ways of framing the question. Alternating between the question of whether life takes priority over profit, which admits a clear logical solution, and the question of how best to exercise care and avoid hurt, in this situation—a question that requires moral imagination—she concludes that there is no single right answer: "I don't think you can say what's right and what's wrong in this situation."

Jake at 11 explained the logical priority of life over law and property by saying that property can be replaced and that the law can make mistakes. At 15, he begins by reiterating the value of life over money ("money sort of comes and goes and human life comes only once") but then imagines the complications that would arise if the druggist had children who were starving. No longer focusing simply on the inexorability of logic, he wonders not only about the druggist's situation but also what Heinz and the druggist are experiencing. Two perspectives are evident as he answers the question, what if the druggist feels strongly about profit? At first he says simply that "he's got the wrong set of priorities" but then approaches the question from a different perspective. Visualizing the situation and considering the feelings evoked by theft and by death, he responds to both feelings at the same time as he judges them to be incommensurate: "I just think what (the druggist) is going to experience is some sorrow and some anger over losing his money, and it's a shame that he's got to feel that, but at the same time that it's a lot, that is not as deplorable a thing as the idea of Heinz, his wife having to die and him having to deal with his wife's dying.'' Suddenly the problem in logic has been joined to a human story.

In terms of their Kohlberg scores at 15 and 11, Amy has gained significantly in moral development, but Jake appears not to have changed. The problems in this unitary representation are apparent when we consider how this judgment of development might affect the two children and their education. By focusing attention only on the adequacy of Amy's justice reasoning and ignoring her other considerations, one equates her development with her ability to accept a construction of reality that she finds problematic. In doing so, one may encourage her to rely on others' definitions and to put aside her own questions as naive or simply irrelevant. For Jake, the focus on justice reasoning would serve to encourage in him the position that anyone who disagreed with his judgments had ''the wrong set of priorities.'' His tempering of this view by imagining and responding to the druggist's experience would go unacknowledged—at worst it would seem to impede his development, at best to be of no moral consequence. The equation of moral development with progress in the justice orientation thus would render Amy more uncertain and Jake more dogmatic. But it also would support the equation of moral education with education for justice, leaving considerations of care untutored. Set apart from the stream of development, these considerations would come to sound increasingly naive and untested as considerations of justice become increasingly practiced and more sophisticated.

To educate both moral voices and represent both orientations in the mapping of human growth means to relinquish the comfort of a single right answer and the clarity of a single road in life. Yet if the opposite of the one is not the many but rather two lines that can be untangled, the prospect of chaos yields to a new way of envisioning development and a new set of questions. Among these questions are those pertaining to the interplay of the lines and the dialogue of the voices— the circumstances in which this dialogue is heard and the conditions in which it is silenced. The tension created by two voices that speak differently about human relationships, we can see a way of speaking about differences without reducing them to the terms of invidious comparison. Then it becomes possible to ask about the origins of these voices in the experience of relationships and to explore the persisting puzzle of why they appear differentially in association with gender.

REMAPPING DEVELOPMENT

In the opening pages of his book *Attachment,* John Bowlby (1969) advises his reader that ''the point of view from which this work starts is different. . . . The change in perspective is radical'' (p. 3). The radical change in perspective is a change in the perspective on relationships, a shift in the focus of attention from the inequality to the attachment of child and parent. Observing in children's responses to loss a capacity for love previously unimagined, Bowlby describes how the presence of this capacity in childhood transforms the account of human development. As he traces the formation of attachment to care-giving and responsiveness in relationships, he renders the process of connection visible as a process of mutual engagement. Proceeding from a different standpoint of observation and presupposing a different set of values, Bowlby aligns development with the strengthening of the capacity to love and measures growth in the ability to survive loss and separation without detachment. From this perspective, development hinges not on the achievement of separation but on the experience of attachment and the ability to sustain this experience through its symbolic representation.

It is notable that Bowlby's insights were gained by entering a world known mainly by women, the world of early childhood vulnerability to experiences of loss and separation. Although the moral implications of this knowledge are in one sense apparent, these implications have not been integrated into theories of human development. Instead the focus on the inequality of child and parent has been so insistent that the insights of attachment theory have been assimilated to concerns about equality and justice. The values of autonomy, objectivity, fairness, and rights are so deeply etched in the psychological imagination that development continues to be traced as a move from inequality to equality, dependence to autonomy, constraint to cooperation. As the radical implications of an alternative vision yield to this unifying perspective, the experience of love itself becomes cast in the language of object relations.

The present remapping of development begins by differentiating two dimensions that characterize all human relationships: the dimension of inequality/equality and the dimension of attachment/detachment (Gilligan, in press). Because both dimensions of relationship are inherent in the connection of parent and child, given the difference between them in size and power and the shared vulnerability created by the attachment necessary for the child's survival, the experiences of inequality and attachment are universal in human life. Although the distinction between these dimensions of relationships appears in the ideals of justice and care to which they give rise as well as in the two modes of self-definition that they imply, their differences are most sharply focused by the two opposites of the word *dependence*.

Because dependence connotes the experience of attachment, its parameters extend along the two coordinates of relationships—leading in one direction to independence and in the other to isolation. The contrasting oppositions of dependence—to independence and to isolation—illuminate different ways of experiencing relationships—as impeding the development of autonomy and as protecting against isolation. Thus in contrast to the prevailing opposition between dependence and independence or autonomy in theories of human development and in the instruments of psychological assessment, the opposition of dependence to isolation informs an alternative vision, transforming the understanding of relationships not only in childhood but also in adolescence.

The two opposites of the word dependence emerged in an ongoing study of female adolescence, appearing in girls' responses to the questions, "What does dependence mean to you?" The study, which is being conducted at a day and boarding school for girls in upstate New York, was designed to map the terrain of female experience that remains uncharted in the literature on adolescence. The question about dependence was asked in the context of a research interview that included questions about past experience, self-description, moral conflicts, and future expectations, appearing at the end of a section about experiences of important relationships. The following examples illustrate the sharp contrast between the view of relationships conveyed by the opposition between dependence and independence and the portrayal that emerges from the opposition of dependence and isolation.

(WHAT DOES DEPENDENCE MEAN TO YOU?)

> I think it is just when you can be dependent on or you can depend on someone, and if you depend on someone, you can depend on them to do certain things, like *to be there* when you need them, and you can depend on people *to understand* your problems, and on the other hand, people can depend on you to do the same thing.

> When you know that *someone is there* when you are upset, and if you need someone *to talk to,* they are there, and you can depend on them *to understand.*

> Well, sometimes it bothers me, the word, because it means that you are depending on somebody to make things happen. But also that you are depending on somebody else *to help you,* you know, either to make things happen for you that are good or just *to be there* when you need them *to talk to* and not feel that you are cutting into their time or that they don't want you there.

> I wouldn't say total dependence but if we ever needed each other for anything, we could totally be dependent on the person and it would be no problem. For me, it means that if I have a problem, I can depend on her *to help me* or anything I need help with, she will *be there to help, whether she can help me or not, she will try,* and the same goes for me.

> That I know if I go to her with a problem or something like that or not a problem but just to see her, even if she has changed and even if I have changed, that we will be able *to talk to* each other.

> Dependence, well, in this case it would be just like I really depend on him *to listen* to me when I have something to say or when I have something I want to talk about, I really want him *to be there* and *to listen* to me.

In these responses dependence is assumed as part of the human condition, and the recurrent phrases, "to be there," "to help," "to talk to," "to listen," convey the perception that people rely on one another for understanding, comfort, and support. Focusing on their needs for others, not construed as a compromise of their integrity, these girls also describe the obligation to be there for others and listen to them. The absence of opposition between dependence and independence is striking in the following response where the two words comingle, conveying a view of independence as enhancing and enhanced by relationships and defining a view of development as occurring through friendship, loyalty, love, and engagement:

> I would say we depend on each other in a way that we are both independent, and I would say we are very independent but as far as our friendship goes, we are dependent on each other because we know that both of us realize that whenever we need something, the other person will always be there.

Thus in contrast to the use of the word dependence to connote hanging from someone like a ball on a string—an object governed by the laws of physics—these girls use the word to convey the perception that attachments arise from the human capacity to move others and to be moved by them. Being dependent, then, no longer means being helpless, powerless, and without control, but rather signifies the knowledge that one is able to have an effect on others, as well as the recognition that the interdependence of attachment empowers both the self and the other, rather than one at the other's expense. The activities of care—being there, listening, the willingness to help, and the ability to understand—take on a moral dimension, reflecting the injunction to pay attention and not to turn away from need. As the knowledge that others are capable of care renders them lovable rather than merely reliable, so the willingness and the ability to care become a standard of self-evaluation.

This portrayal of care, nurturance, and affiliation reveals their cognitive as well as affective dimensions, their foundation in the ability to perceive people in their own terms and to respond to their needs. As such knowledge generates the power both to help and to hurt, the uses of this power become the measure of responsibility and care in relationships. In adolescence, when the advent of puberty and the growth of subjective and reflective thought change the experience of self and relationships, girls describe conflicts between their responsibilities to themselves and their responsibility to others. Seeking to perceive and respond to their own as well as to others' needs, they ask if they can be responsive to themselves without losing connection to others and whether they can respond to others without abandoning themselves. This search for an inclusive solution to these dilemmas of loyalty vies with the tendency toward exclusion expressed through the moral opposition between selfish and selfless choice—an opposition where selfishness connotes the exclusion of others and selflessness the exclusion of self. Thus the themes of inclusion and exclusion, salient in the childhood games girls play, come to be addressed consciously in adolescence, defining a line of identity and moral development that leads through changes in the experience and understanding of attachment.

Within this framework of relationships, the central metaphor for identity formation becomes the metaphor of dialogue rather than that of mirroring. The emphasis on speaking and listening, on being heard and making oneself understood, ties self-definition to an active engagement with others and turns attention to the process of communication. The themes of silence and voice that emerge so centrally in girls' descriptions convey the struggle to claim a voice and to find an opening that allows the subjectively known self to enter into relationship. But with others, the imagery of silence and silencing also conveys girls' recognition of how readily this process can be foiled when the refusal to listen creates an impression of coming up against a wall. Although silence can be a way of maintaining integrity in the face of such disconfirmation—a way of avoiding invalidation—the willingness to speak and risk disagreement is central to the process of adolescent engagement, making possible the reweaving and attachment and the transformation of relationships.

"I just wish to become better in my relationship with my mother, to be able more easily to disagree with her" . . . and this wish to engage with others on one's own terms rather than seeking connection by "making myself in their image" signifies both the temptation to yield to others' perceptions and the recognition that the exclusion of self like the exclusion of others renders relationships lifeless by dissolving the fabric of connection. Given the failure of interpretive schemes to reflect female experience and given the celebration of selflessness as the virtue of feminine assessment, development for girls in adolescence hinges on their willingness to challenge two equations: the equation of human with male and the equation of care with self-sacrifice. Both these equations in conjunction have sustained a unitary conception of human development and a problematic conception of human relationships.

By bringing a new imagery of relationships to the depiction of adolescent development, by tying identity formation to dialogue and morality to care and responsiveness in relationships, the study of female experience enlarges existing theoretical conceptions by filling in a line that has been missing from accounts of human development. The representation of relationships along the two dimensions of inequality/equality and attachment/detachment informs two ways of describing the path of development . . . as a linear progression from inequality to equality, achieved by climbing a staircase of stages and as an elaboration of attachment or interdependence achieved by strengthening connection and resisting detachment. As the concept of gender stands as a symbol of inequality and as a symbol of interdependence, the asymmetry of gender in early family relationships suggests why these two images of inequality and interdependence tend to have differential salience in male and female experience (see Chodorow,

1978). At the same time, the study of gender differences calls attention to the need to represent both of these images of relationships in the account of human development.

Vygotsky (1978), describing the process of internalization through which higher psychological functions develop, notes that these functions—voluntary attention, logical memory, and concept formation—originate as actual relations between human individuals. In the course of development, "an interpersonal process is transformed into an intrapersonal one" (p. 57). The remapping of development proposed here extends Vigotsky's description by delineating two dimensions of interpersonal connection that imply different concepts and different ways of thinking. This more differentiated portrayal of relationships changes the account of identity and moral development and transforms the understanding of a series of relationships that have been imagined along a single dimension. By envisioning the connections between parent and child, teacher and student, therapist and patient, researcher and subject not only in terms of their inequality but also in terms of their attachment, it becomes possible to see how the parent is nurtured by the child, how the teacher learns from the student, how the therapist is healed by the patient, and how the researcher is informed by the subject. The moral implications of this change in perception are joined by the recognition that this vision generates a conception of development that provides a better mapping of human experience.

ACKNOWLEDGMENTS

The research discussed in this chapter was supported by grants from the Spencer Foundation, the Milton Fund, the small grants section of the National Institute for Mental Health, the National Institute of Education, the Geraldine Rockefeller Dodge Foundation, and by a generous gift from Marilyn Brachman Hoffman. I am indebted to Mrs. Hoffman and also to Scott McVay and Valerie Peed of the Dodge Foundation for their interest and encouragement, and I am grateful to the Carnegie Corporation for enabling me to spend a year as a faculty fellow at the Bunting Institute of Radcliffe College.

REFERENCES

Bettelheim, B. (1977). *The uses of enchantment*. New York: Vintage Books.

Blum, L. (1980). *Friendship, altruism and morality*. Boston: Routledge & Kegan Paul.

Bowlby, J. (1969, 1973, 1980). *Attachment and loss*. New York: Basic Books, three volumes.

Chodorow, N. (1978). *The reproduction of mothering*. Berkeley, CA: University of California Press.

Colby, A., Kohlberg, L. Candee, D., Gibbs, J., Hewer, A., Speicher, B. (1985). *The measurement of moral judgment: A manual and its results*. New York: Cambridge University Press.

Gilligan, C. (1982). *In a different voice: Psychological theory and women's development*. Cambridge, MA: Harvard University Press.

Gilligan, C. (1984, Summer) The conquistador and the dark continent: Reflections on the psychology of love. *Daedalus,* 75–95.

Gilligan, C. (in press). Remapping the moral domain: New images of the self in relationship. In T. C. Heller, M. Sosna, & D. Wellbery (Eds.), *Reconstructing individualism: Autonomy, individuality, and the self in western thought.* Stanford, CA: Stanford University Press.

Gilligan, C., Langdale, S., Lyons, N., & Murphy, J. M. (1982). *The contribution of women's thought to developmental theory.* Report to the National Institute of Education. Cambridge, MA: Harvard University.

Hoffman, M. (1976). Empathy, role taking guilt, and development of altruistic motives. In T. Lickona (Ed.), *Moral development and behavior.* New York: Holt, Rinehart, & Winston.

Johnston, D. K. (1985). *Two moral orientations—two problem-solving strategies: Adolescents' solutions to dilemmas in fables.* Unpublished doctoral dissertation, Harvard University, School of Education.

Kohlberg, L. (1969). Stage and sequence: The cognitive-developmental approach to socialization. In D. A. Goslin (Ed.), *Handbook of socialization theory and research.* Chicago: Rand McNally.

Kohlberg, L. (1981, 1984). *Essays on moral development. Vols. 1 & 2: The philosophy of moral development, The psychology of moral development.* San Francisco: Harper & Row.

Langdale, S. (1983). *Moral orientations and moral development: The analysis of care and justice reasoning across different dilemmas in females and males from childhood to adulthood.* Unpublished doctoral dissertation, Harvard University, School of Education.

Lyons, N. (1980). *Seeing the consequences.* Unpublished qualifying paper, Harvard University.

Lyons, N. (1982). *Conceptions of self and morality and modes of moral choice.* Unpublished doctoral dissertation, Harvard University, School of Education.

Lyons, N. (1983, May). Two perspectives: On self, relationships and morality. *Harvard Educational Review,* 125–145.

Vygotsky, L. S. (1978). *Mind in society.* M. Cole, V John-Steiner, S. Scribner, E. Souberman (Eds.), Cambridge & London: Harvard University Press.

DISCUSSION

WARTOFSKY: I'd like to start with a devil's advocate question. Suppose it's true, as you say, that here are these elements from women's experience which don't show up in the male dominant development models that prevail. On the other hand, women's experience is generated from a situation of being dominated. If that situation were to change and if one's character changes with one's situation, then if women become prime ministers they may end up waging war in the Falklands.

GILLIGAN: And get re-elected.

WARTOFSKY: And get re-elected. It's not entirely clear what to infer from that. Would it be that if male domination were changed, women's experience and men's experience would change in such a way that neither of these orientations would persist, even as alternatives?

There might be either some melding of them or unforeseen forms of experience which could then be developmental models. Or is there, instead, some notion that, precisely because of the situation of domination, *that* experience has called forth certain values and characteristics which would be normatively good to include in developmental models? If we are talking about value presuppositions of development, we are presumably saying that it is these elements out of women's experience which now ought to be included in our norms of development which we are therefore putting forth as policy, as Jerome Bruner proposed. That's the gist of the question.

GILLIGAN: It's a marvelous question because it clarifies my central point that there is a distinction between two dimensions of relationships. One is inequality, characterizing relationships in terms of dominance and subordination; and the other, interdependence, which generates a different image of human connection. I was not arguing that one is better than the other. I was arguing that both of these dimensions are embedded in the cycle of human life, that both males and females have had the experience, at least as children, of being both unequal and interdependent. I suggested that our developmental theories have emphasized one dimension and have neglected the other and that this emphasis leads to the casting of all problems as problems of dominance and subordination. I wanted to call attention to the failure to represent the other dimension of relationships and [to] argue that one cannot assimilate these two experiences of relationships to a single mode. My argument was that current stages of human development have made that assimilation. It never quite works, which is why you have that confusion in Kohlberg's Stage III and why intimacy sits, oddly, in the middle of Erikson's sequence of stages. At the end of a sequence of stages in Erikson that all work toward the development of autonomy, suddenly, out of nowhere, comes intimacy. In other words, the two voices I described are heard and understood by both sexes. You talk about interdependence; men know about interdependence. If you talk about inequality, women know about that, although, in certain situations they won't speak of it or they may not even recognize it. My central point, in that sense, was perfectly illustrated by your question which is the move immediately to construct the problem in terms of dominance and subordination.

The tentativeness, if you like, of my own present formulation is that the dimension of interdependence really has not been explored. Even studies of children's social relationships, social perspective taking, social cognitive development—if you follow the progression of stages you'll see that progress is always marked in the capacity to be more autonomous (more bounded), to transform relationships from a hierarchical to a contractual mode. The interesting thing about the dimension of interdependence, the other orientation, is it *presumes* connection. The significance of that presumption is that you can't look at development except always of a person in relation to somebody else.

If I can take another minute, I'll show the problem that females have posed for theories of human development. It is very difficult to tell a single story about child development given the asymmetry of gender relations in the family. Freud noticed this in 1914 in his paper "On Narcissism" and, in a sense, got rid of the problem by saying simply that females didn't develop. That's one solution. But you see why that's such an appealing solution. Because to say females develop, then you have to have an account of development that can represent this asymmetry of relationships.

If you take Vygotsky's notion, concepts arise initially in an interpersonal situation and then become intrapersonal, the differences in the interpersonal situation may have some effect, by which I don't mean binding effect or eternal effect, but some effect on the kinds of concepts formed. Nancy Chodorow's work that points out how the formation of gender identity has a different dynamic in the context of the relationship to a person of the same or opposite sex—in relationship to the mother the male child must define himself as male by separating, the female child defines herself as female through that connection—would suggest that on the dimension of identity certain differences will tend to recur in male and female personality formation.

These two dimensions of interdependence and inequality-equality, the very difference in the way you define them suggests that the structure is different. One has two poles; the other doesn't. You can transfer from the analysis of the family to the analysis of society, as has been done in [the] contrast of Gesellschaft and Gemeinschaft. Again, my argument would be it's not that one is in one domain and the other is in the other domain—justice in the public sphere, care in the home—but rather these two dimensions are in both domains. The failure to represent both dimensions, or the tendency to see women's experience as somehow uninteresting or unimportant in the account of development, as though the interaction between thought and experience didn't include these experiences, reflects exactly the tendency which appeared in your question, which is again an interesting question but doesn't address the other mode.

One final comment. Yes, it's true. If people move into structures of hierarchy that are organized around dominance and subordination, they will think increasingly, particularly as they seek power, about issues of justice and rights. The increasing movement of women into these structures currently, I think, generates a tension between the extent to which it will pull women's thinking more into that mode or the extent to which women, given their greater experience of interdependence, may help to transform those structures so that they are less distancing and destructive of caring relationships.

KAGAN: Carol, you made your case persuasively. Could we tempt you to confess your private instincts as to the contribution of historically conditioned facts to these two voices. That is, is it your belief that women have been in a less subordinate position [or do] you believe that, in addition, there are some powerful universals in childhood that make it easier for women of all cultures to adopt their voice?

GILLIGAN: Do I believe there are universals in human development that will predispose females toward this mode? Certainly. The capacity of females to bear children gives them an easier access to the fact of interdependence, whether or not they have children because each female is a child of a female who had a child. So, there's that knowledge that comes more readily of the self as interdependent because of the biology of reproduction as well as the different dynamics of gender identity formation. I think that because we have been so inattentive to female experience, so ready to dismiss it as instinctual or irrelevant to theories of human development, we have no idea how prevalent this understanding of interdependence is in males. Now I think that's a very open research question. The work I did with women led me to see aspects of male thinking that were absolutely not represented. So that's one question.

But the second is a more strictly historical question. At the present time the limits of the concept of autonomy and the dangers in working from a model of equality and inequality—I just think of the missile gap, the arms race, and so forth—have become increasingly apparent. In a nuclear age, in a world where the ecology is threatened by pollution, autonomy becomes a very dangerous illusion. The notion of autonomy on an historical level—the enlightenment project, the notion of nation states, and so forth—finds its parallel in psychology in the conception of the individual as an autonomous self. Historically, this may be a time when we must look for sources of a different vision, not only in philosophy and theory but also in the fabric of human development. From this perspective, if female development is privileged in its access to this understanding, then female development becomes extremely interesting at this time. Not so much simply to repair or undo a previous inequity but to inform ways of thinking about human growth that really can apply to both of the sexes.

KAGAN: How important do you think this is as a determining factor? As you know, if you ask 5-year-old children from many cultures who is stronger, who is more potent, who is more dangerous, children of both sexes will say the male. I've always believed that something happens to young boys and girls. There are only two life agenda that can be followed: one of power and one of interdependence. Girls decide early that the power agenda cannot be pursued as a primary goal, so they follow what you call the female voice. How important is that?

GILLIGAN: All right, let me respond again by noting the nature of the question. If you ask children who is more powerful, in a sense you are asking them to think. . . .

KAGAN: Yes, but asked the other way around, they'll do it the same way. If you ask them who's gentler or who's softer, boys will say female. It works both ways. It's symmetrical for both sexes.

GILLIGAN: All right, but that's interesting, because cognitively we understand the answer to the first question just simply in terms of the assimilation of the dimensions of size and power. As long as males are bigger we'll understand why children will say they are more powerful. Hopefully, with development, this immature mode of cognition changes . . . [Laughter and applause] . . . unless, of course, it becomes so reinforced as to become social reality.

The question would be very interesting to me, to know 5-year-olds' answers as to why females are more caring. The tentativeness I feel is because of my acute awareness of how many questions we have never asked. If we proceed to theory on the basis of only the questions we ask, we keep representing over and over again a set of premises and a single dimension of relationship. Focusing on females' caring, asking that question myself, I came to an interesting view of the female child which is very different from the usual view in the literature. The young child is often described as a naturalist exploring the physical world, which is then, as Jerry Bruner indicated, taken as the model for the social world—I think a problematic transposition. The child is classifying animals and minerals, and so forth and so on. I think of the female child as a naturalist in the social world—collecting information, performing experiments, making a series of observations which then, around the age of 11, tend to become transformed into a series of theoretical or if-then statements. If you do this to this person, then this is likely to happen. These are testable hypotheses. If you ask, again an unasked question, how come sixth-grade girls know so much about what is going on in the sixth-grade classroom? Where have they learned this? How do they know it? What have they attended to? What have they perceived? and so forth, then you can not only think of this question in the terms of what Jerry Kagan mentioned, but you can also begin to think what are the kinds of activities that would lead to the capacity to care, to the awareness of what constitutes hurt, and trace a pattern of growth that hinges on changing understandings through experience of what is care and what is hurt, a more psychologically complex hypothesis.

BERNSTEIN: There is something that I find perplexing. It's in the book, it's in the talk, it's in your responses. I have never quite figured how specific and local and historically conditioned your claims are, how universal they are. I want to ask the same question from several different perspectives. One way of looking at what is wrong with some theories of moral development is how the whole field has been guided by a model which we know is historically oriented. When you speak about ''autonomy,'' you're not speaking about autonomy, you're speaking about a certain conception of autonomy, and when you're speaking about justice, and you're speaking about rights. We know that this is something which has occurred only in the modern period. We know that there is a dark side of this, a hidden side of domination, and this is something we should have known since Marx. We can now take this as well entrenched and as characteristic of male thinking. One can always ask, ''Well, aren't you really telling us something about the role of a dominant ideology in the 20th century, at best, and a kind of counter-ideology?'' That's one way of asking the question.

Another way of asking the same question is as philosopher, on a theoretical level. When you begin speaking about models of interdependence and care, this has been older than the tradition of rights and justice. We forget that the major part of Aristotle's ethics was about friendship and the forms of friendship and the forms of coming together. In a way, we can read the whole Hegelian-Marxist tradition as in some ways emphasizing, at a theoretical level, the dark side of the one voice that you're talking about and clarifying what a genuine community would be. When you make the kind of allusions, analogous in the book, to parent–child relations, and so forth, there's the suggestion that it is somehow more deeply embedded, more structurally embedded, and yet it seems to me you then at other times say, ''No, no, I don't want to go that far. It's good enough for me simply to note that at least right now we have these different voices, these different perspectives, and that we really have to listen to both of them.'' It's on this issue—which seems to me to plague a good deal of developmental psychology, what in old Marxist terminology would be called reification, moving from something specific, local, to the lure of universality—I'm never quite clear where you stand.

GILLIGAN: Let me start at the beginning. [Laughter]

BERNSTEIN: That's going to take a long time.

GILLIGAN: No, [the beginning] of your question. Am I referring to something specific and local or do I mean to imply universality? I do begin with particular observations made in a limited context to raise a series of questions and ask about their presence at this particular historical time. I was interested in the resonance of these observations to observations made in other periods, and I used literature as a way of both amplifying the voices I had heard and indicating that aspects of these voices were not limited to the particular period in the local context. One way the enlightenment project can be understood as it arose against the social fabric that was much more interdependent and connected, it arose in opposition to that, to criticize the dark side of connection; it began to erode and destroy that fabric. What we see historically now is the re-emergence of those voices. In this culture it says, ''We have lost something that we must reconstruct.'' This makes enormous sense to me because my own vision of these two voices is that they must be in dialogue with each other; that they must correct each other. And that is why I start with this premise of these two dimensions built into relationships. Interdependence doesn't remove the fact of inequality, the potential for domination, and so forth. You might have shifts over history as one tends to get lost and maybe each one loses the other. Sometimes I think of these as a figure-ground problem. Think of the word *dependence* and the two opposites—*independence* and *isolation*. Your feelings shift as you move from one axis to the other. You oppose dependence and independence, you feel relationships are constraining, closing you in, hemming you in. You move from dependence to isolation, you start thinking, ''How can I maintain these connections?'' There is a real emotional ambivalence, not internal in the individual but coming right out of this figure-ground shift in relationships.

The final observation is that whether one starts with Aristotle or any period in history, the absence of women's voices from the human record is continuous. There is a question in my mind as to whether the understanding of interdependence changes from thinking of it as a societal fabric, Gemeinschaft, whether that concept is enriched and made more specific and grounded when you think of it in terms of women's experience and their sense of the intrinsic connection between other and self. You see how it changes the moral problem if you see self and other as connected. If you hurt others, you hurt yourself; if you hurt yourself, you hurt others. There's not a simple zero-sum opposition; rather, there's no way out of the ramification, resonance, of action through a narrative of relationship. The abortion situation is a perfect example because choice then doesn't become an isolated moment. Choice is embedded in a narrative sequence of events which is a sequence of relationships. There is no way to do nothing. The pregnant woman, if she has an abortion, has an abortion, and if she doesn't she has a child. So action is inescapable. The whole perspective of what is a moral problem, what is choice, what is action, changes. That's why I come back to the evidence of women.

AUDIENCE MEMBER: There are lots of questions I would like to discuss, but one, I think, is a matter of frequent misunderstanding and that is that you are not speaking about women. In some ways women lean more to what you are saying, whatever the reason, and I have a different reason for it. Namely, I'd take very much into account the situation in society, and this is a characteristic I would ascribe at least to the old people who are in the position of being devaluated in society. The two orientations are pretty much the same. That means it is the position of being devaluated or looked down [on] which gives you a very different view of the world and especially on interpersonal relationships. This is a problem with the position of being dominated, you want to say, or being devaluated, as we have it.

GILLIGAN: Two quick responses. First, trying to keep these dimensions separate rather than fuse them with one another and see interdependence as something that is only known by subordinates in a society, let me give one explanation as to why if one is going to rise to domination, it depends on distancing. One is comfortable as the dominant only if one is less aware of the subordinate's feelings. So, the very move into the dimension of inequality is going to diminish the connection to the other person.

The second point derives from some observations of young children. It is the experience of caring for others that enables one, in a sense, to know about care and receive care from them. So, again, I look to the activities that lead to this other orientation in its own terms. But the final point about women—I assume that women are human. Human has been equated with the male, so we talk about human development and about women as some separate group. I assume that knowing about women can tell us something about humans. Therefore, I haven't talked at all today about what I would say if I was talking about women as a group, what problems they face, and so forth. Half the population has not been studied. There may be in this group some insights into human behavior, just as we have learned things that tell us about women from the studies that we have done with men.

AUDIENCE MEMBER: May I just make one remark? The same argument can be said about people who are devaluated in our society. I am working with the elderly and there is the same kind of situation, and you can take minority groups and other things and you will have similar approaches. In other words, I am only suggesting that it should not be limited to women.

GILLIGAN: On, no, I agree with you.

4 Presuppositions in Developmental Inquiry

Jerome Kagan
Harvard University

A meeting devoted to philosophical matters at a time when psychology is being nibbled to death by biology may strike some as "fiddling." But I think our failure to make as much progress as we and our patrons expected is partly attributable to presuppositions about terms and empirical procedures that need to be examined. If social scientists make explicit the suppositions that guide their empirical work, perhaps the resulting debate will facilitate conceptual clarity and create a sense of progress. The first two of the seven premises considered in this chapter are primitives; hence, they are stated succinctly and without argument. They do not have a popular alternative at the present time, although they did in the past. The remaining five assumptions are controversial because each has a legitimate complement, and both propositions are occasionally evaluated by formal analysis and research. As a result, the degree of commitment each alternative enjoys is affected by argument and evidence, and is considered in detail. My defense of one of the alternatives relies more on data than on authority or formal argument. That choice is not intended to minimize the persuasive force of elegant essays by wise scholars, but reflects the fact that in my experience phenomena have been the more useful guide to suppositions.

THE PRESUPPOSITIONS

On Existence. I assume that events exist outside of an observer's experience, and that agents' perceptions of these events will not be identical across species and will even vary among individuals of a particular species. I am persuaded by Russell's assertion that the part of the earth's surface where Edinburgh now stands is north of the part where London stands, even if no person knows about north and south and there are no minds in the universe (Russell, 1912).

A belief in the reality of objects is so strong that five-month-old infants will become distressed if they reach for an arrangement of light that appears to be an object but, because it is only an image, offers no feeling of solidity when their fingers contact the light (Starkey, 1983).

On Relatedness.   I assume that occasionally events are not independent of one another; there are repeatable covariations among the occurrences of specific events.

On Description.   The symbolic descriptions of events and the names for the inferred relations between non-simultaneous events (sometimes called constructs) that comprise scientific knowledge are always incomplete. They capture only part of the event and only an aspect of the relation among events. The poverty of the symbolic description is partly attributable to the fact that the empirical procedure that provides the relevant information necessarily reveals only a portion of the event (or events) to be understood. The position of empiricists is much like that of two blind persons, one with scissors and the other with a jackknife, who, after being told the characteristics of a rose petal, are instructed to find one and to separate it from its surroundings so that the product is perfectly faithful to the original petal. Even if our blind adventurers should be fortunate enough to find a rose bush, it is unlikely that they would cut away one complete petal and nothing more. Each would probably detach part of a petal, part of a stem, and perhaps a bit of the bush and return with their non-identical products convinced that each had found the perfect rose petal.

Contemporary psychology suffers from the fact that investigators use different procedures to measure what each believes is the same property and are indifferent to the likelihood that the resulting descriptions do not have identical meanings. The physicist Freeman Dyson writes, "it is hopeless to look for a description independent of the mode of observation" (1979, p. 249). When 18th-century observers made a statement about a child's lability or fear, their colleagues knew that the source of the statement was the child's overt behavior, for this was the method of choice. Today, investigators use questionnaires, interviews, memory performance, and polygraphic display of changes in heart rate or patterns of neural discharge to evaluate these states. Even if we ignore the fact that these methods might not evaluate lability or fear with accuracy, scientists make statements about the degree to which a child possesses these and other properties, and ignore the real possibility that because the measurement methods are different the propositions are not equivalent.

Imagine an investigator at the end of the 18th century who noted that soybean plants grow taller if they are exposed to sunlight, and wrote that the energy contained in sunlight makes soybean plants grow. The modern botanist does different experiments because he knows that the plant's cells convert the sunlight into chemical energy. He states that the energy contained in the plant's cells makes soybean plants grow. Does the word *energy* in the two explanations have the same meaning? The answer is not quite, for the forms the energy assumes—photons or chemical bonds—are far from similar, even though contemporary physicists assume that a single abstract essence of energy lies behind the two forms. Because the less mature sciences have few, if any, theoretically useful abstract essences, it will be wise initially to frame constructs in terms of the varied forms inferred from different procedures, rather than posit abstract essences. I am not persuaded that psychology has discovered any valid essences. These are prizes gained at the end of a long investigative journey when sets of reliable relations require such abstractions. The sciences of human nature have not yet earned that privilege.

A second important difference between the physical sciences and the sciences of human nature concerns the form of the statements that describe relations among events. Each scholar wants to determine the truth value of statements with the form, "If A, then B," whether A and B refer to current flow and voltage or famine and revolution. Further, most want these statements to be as free as possible of conditions that must be actualized if the relation between A and B is to hold, for they recognize that all such statements should be written contingently as, "If A, then B, if X, Y, and Z." Obviously, one can rewrite the latter statement as, "If A and X and Y and Z, then B." The preference for the first form over the second separates the physical sciences and some parts of the biological sciences from most of the behavioral and social sciences.

The physicist typically controls the constraining conditions—for example, pressure, temperature, or resistance—plucks out the functional relation of primary interest, and states it is a maximally generalizable law. The psychologist, by contrast, is more often interested in how the constraining conditions affect the relation between A and B. This is not surprising, for the greater the variability inherent in the consequent events, the more significant the constraining conditions are likely to be. Living forms have a degree of variability that far exceeds that of inorganic materials. Thus, behavioral scientists ask interesting questions about the role of constraining conditions that physicists find far less intriguing.

Each discipline names its constraining conditions differently. In social psychology they refer to the context; in linguistics, the intention of the speaker and the frame of the listener; in developmental psychology, the knowledge and emotional state of the child. I prefer to insert these constraints in the noun phrase rather than as a tag at the end of the generalization. I prefer, "If an 8-month-old who is temperamentally prone to become fearful encounters a stranger who approaches quietly and in an unnatural way, the infant will show signs of anxiety,'' to ''Eight-month-old infants will show signs of anxiety to a stranger if they are temperamentally prone to become fearful, and the stranger approaches quietly and in an unnatural way.'' The second proposition is usually preferred because it has the illusion of generality.

The choice of one construction over the other is part of a larger tension that monitors the selection of psychological constructs. How general or specific should psychological terms be? A majority of psychologists continue to prefer constructs of maximal generality that mute the effects of setting, incentive, and target.

Discussions of the differences between competence and performance in essays on cognitive development provide an illustration of the popular tendency to assume broad rather than narrow competences. Close analysis reveals a fuzzy quality to the construct of competence. One must distinguish first between the ability to use knowledge or a talent a person already possesses—an actual competence—and the ability to acquire new skills, operations, or information—a potential competence. An actual competence is a person's ability to remember the name of a close friend. The competence in this case is quite specific—''knowledge of the name of a person.'' The competence does not include the ability to recall the names of people in general and certainly does not refer to anything as broad as the competence to remember all classes of verbal information.

Psychologists use a failure in performance to infer an incomplete, immature, or flawed competence. But this inference is often vulnerable. When a child or adult fails a problem—let us say, a 10-year-old cannot recall a list of six unrelated words—we do not know whether the poor performance was due to failure to use an actual competence (the child knew and registered the names but was not motivated to recall them), or to a flaw in the potential competence to register the sequence of unrelated words. The latter failure could be due to lack of knowledge of the meanings of some of the words, not knowing how to rehearse them, not being able to focus attention, or a host of other abilities.

But suppose that we were able, through careful experimentation, to diagnose the exact nature of the fragile competence. How general a name should we give it? Assume that the inferior performance was due to an imperfection of the potential competence to focus attention on each word as it was being read. It is highly unlikely that this child would be unable to pay attention to all verbal information on all occasions, and just as improbable that the impaired competence is limited to this particular set of words. Elimination of those two admittedly extreme alternatives leaves an enormous space in which to find the best description of the child's ''lack of competence.''

This hypothetical example contains the essence of the controversy surrounding the concept competence. Some prefer to enlarge the domain of the competence; others wish to narrow it. I favor a restricted conception because existing data imply that nature is usually very particular. Mayan Indian 8-year-olds living in the northwest highlands of Guatemala have great difficulty remembering a series of familiar but unrelated words or pictures. Despite many trials and a patient indigenous examiner, most children could not recall more than three or four words, when after each series of one length was mastered, an additional word or picture was added to the series just memorized. American children of the same age can remember a series of 12 words or 12 pictures under similar testing conditions. Mayan Indian children seem to lack the potential competence to register and to retrieve verbal and pictorial information across a half dozen different memory tasks. The consistency of this performance tempts us to regard the competence failure as being broad in scope. But when these same children were required to learn to associate 20 unique geometric designs with 20 different meaningful words, they learned these arbitrary pairs quickly and efficiently. Apparently there was something about this particular task that was friendly to their abilities, and it would be incorrect to posit a competence as broad as recall memory for symbolic information (Kagan, Klein, Finley, Rogoff, & Nolan, 1979).

In young disciplines, scientific advance often turns out to be the discovery of the limits of a process that had been over-extended. Pasteur and Jenner found that very specific forms of life spoiled wine and produced human illness—effects that had been attributed to very broad forces. It is likely that most of the currently popular potential competences, like intelligence, spatial ability, or even imagery, are much too broad, and future research will reveal their proper and more limited sphere of operation.

On Categories versus Continua.   It is useful to conceive of some constructs as qualitative categories rather than as continua. Psychologists typically prefer variables that are quantified as a continuous metric (reaction time, number of errors, heart rate). When investigators discover a relation between two such variables—let us say, between prolonged reaction times and few errors to a test that has response uncertainty   they prefer to assume that the quality implied by the relation is a graded dimension, with each subject capable of being assigned a position on the continuum. But note the error in assuming an underlying continuum in the relation between body temperature and changes in the circulatory system. Physiologists tell us that special processes generated when body temperature rises above 99 degrees are not actualized when the body temperature is between 98 and 99 degrees.

This theme has been a persistent source of debate among philosophers and scientists. On the one hand, we have Aristotle's insistence on discrete qualities and, on the other, Plato's view that the surface characteristics that comprise experience are derived from continuities of more basic elements. The status and power of mathematics, which were enhanced in the subsequent two millenia, persuaded most Enlightenment scholars to side with Plato and to assume that God used mathematics as the language of nature. Hence, natural phenomena were presumed to rest on a set of continuous functions.

But even though an investigator assigns a continuous set of numbers to represent the frequency, latency, or duration of a particular response, children or adults with high values on a variable might be qualitatively different from those with lower values. Consider two examples from work of our laboratory.

In a recent study of 60 first-born 3-year-olds we found a group of 10 children who, across a series of cognitive procedures, showed a high and very stable heart rate and a group of 11 children who showed a low and very variable heart rate. When these two groups were treated as discrete classes, lawful relations with other qualities emerged. The children with a high and stable heart rate—who might be regarded as having higher sympathetic tone—were more obedient with and vigilant toward the mother, less aggressive with an unfamiliar peer, and more highly motivated on cognitive tasks than the children with low and variable heart rates. The former group seemed to be more effectively socialized with respect to qualities American mothers regard as desirable. However, when we created a continuous variable based on the average standard score for heart rate and heart rate variability (the correlation between these two variables was high), and a second continuous index of obedience, aggression, and cognitive performance, there was no relation for the whole sample between the two continuous variables. Understanding was enhanced if we viewed the two groups of children as being qualitatively different from the rest of the population and avoided assigning each child a position on a continuous quality (Kagan & Reznick, 1984).

A second example comes from our continuing investigations of behavioral inhibition in young children. The initial tendency to withdraw, to seek proximity to the mother, to become quiet, and to be vigilant with an unfamiliar child or adult can be regarded as a continuous quality some might call timidity, shyness, or, as we prefer, inhibition to the unfamiliar. However, the stability of this behavioral quality across the interval 20 to 48 months of age, and its relations with other characteristics, were more robust when we treated the extremes of the distribution as if they represented qualitatively different types of children than when we viewed the quality of inhibition as a continuous trait. Further, even within the group of behaviorally inhibited children it proved useful to divide them into qualitatively different groups. Among 22 children who were all extremely inhibited at 20 months of age, some showed several signs of high sympathetic tone, whereas others did not. These signs included a high and stable heart rate while processing discrepant information and frequent bouts of chronic constipation and sleeplessness during infancy. Other children who were similar in their degree of behavioral inhibition did not show these signs. It is possible to regard these two groups as falling on a continuum some might call, ''intensity of anxiety.'' However, the children who displayed both behavioral inhibition and signs of high sympathetic tone at 20 months were more likely to have many unusual fears and to have remained behaviorally inhibited at age 4 than the behaviorally inhibited children who did not show signs of high sympathetic tone.

It seems more fruitful to conceive of these two groups of children as qualitatively different, rather than assume that each child can be assigned a position on a continuum of anxiety, tension, or fearfulness. I believe that the behaviorally inhibited children with high sympathetic tone are being influenced by biological forces that predispose them to inhibition to the unfamiliar, whereas the other inhibited children may have acquired their behavioral surface as a result of socialization experiences (Kagan, Reznick, Clarke, Snidman, & Coll, 1984).

Connectedness versus Discontinuity.   The preference for positing continuous forces is also present in the assumption of connectedness in human development. Faith in a connectivity between the deep past and the present remains an essential premise in most popular theories of human development, as it has been since the beginning of formal study of the child in the decades following Darwin's great work. Most theorists assume a structural link between all phases of development and write in affirmation of Russell's bold assertion, "The chain of causation can be traced by the inquiring mind from any given point backwards to the creation of the world" (cited in Hanson, 1961, p. 50). Most authors have implied that no part of the child's past could be lost; every psychological property in the adult could, in theory, be traced to a distant origin. In a popular psychology text written in the first decade of this century, Edward L. Thorndike (1905) ended his final chapter with a ringing affirmation of the connectivity between the child's first acquisitions and adult life.

> Though we seem to forget what we learned, each mental acquisition really leaves its mark and makes future judgments more sagacious; . . . . nothing of good or evil is ever lost; we may forget and forgive, but the neurones never forget or forgive. . . . It is certain that every worthy deed represents a modification of the neurones of which nothing can ever rob us. Every event of a man's mental life is written indelibly in the brain's archives, to be counted for or against him. (pp. 330–331)

Piaget (1951) states the same premise in different words.

> Thus, when we study the beginnings of intelligence we were forced to go as far back as the reflex in order to trace the cause of the assimilating activity which finally leads to the construction of adaptive schemas, for it is only by a principle of functional continuity that the indefinite variety of structures can be explained. (p. 6)

Most declarations of connectivity between very early and later stages of development have been based on a single superficial similarity between one aspect of behavior of an infant and an analogous dimension in older children or adults. Havelock Ellis saw a relationship between a nursing infant and adult sexuality. But humans are so adept at inventing theoretical similarities between fundamentally different phenomena, simply by detecting one feature that seems to be shared by the two events, such imaginative creations are hardly sufficient to prove or even imply their true functional relation. A century ago the protesting cry of the 1-year-old following maternal departure was classified as similar to the willful disobedience of the adult. Today the same act is grouped with the anxiety and sadness that follow loss of a sweetheart, spouse, or parent.

There are many reasons why American psychologists are receptive to believing in continuity in development. Such a belief renders original forms useful and rationalizes the maxim that one must prepare for the future. If the future is determined by the present, then it is to some degree knowable through careful attention to each day's action and experience. Further, arguments for connectivity have the illusion of being mechanistic, for if each new function is preceded by another which makes a substantial contribution to it, it seems that one is better able to state the cause-effect sequence than if a function emerges relatively rapidly as a result of a historically recent endogenous change. I also suspect that the premise of connectedness appears to some to be in greater accord with egalitarian principles than the possibility of discontinuous growth, for the latter is likely to be due to maturational changes in the central nervous system. Some believe—I add incorrectly—that any emphasis on the role of biological forces is inconsistent with egalitarian premises. This need not be. The belief in the permanence of characteristics is also helped by our language habits, for English contains a bias favoring continuity in an individual's qualities. The adjectives used to describe young children rarely refer to the age of the actor or to the context of the action. Like the names of colors, they imply a permanence over time and place. Descriptors like passive, irritable, intelligent, or labile are applied to infants, children, and adults as if the meanings of these terms were not altered by growth. This is not true in all languages; in Japanese different words are used to describe the quality of intelligence in a child and adult. There is always a strong temptation to assume that entities with the same name are of the same essence. Sixteenth-century herbalists classified wheat (a grass) with buckwheat (which is not a grass) because both had "wheat" in their names. Simply using the same word to describe a characteristic in children and adults tempts each of us to believe that there is a hidden disposition that survives, unchanged, over the years.

Modern neuroscience has strengthened the 19th-century belief that psychological experiences can be translated into sentences that have purely physiological content. Experience can affect the weight of the brain and early stimulation can add dendritic spines to brain cells and alter the sensitivity of the visual cortex to vertical lines. The belief that experience produces a permanent change in the brain, wedded to the premise that the brain directs thought and behavior, implies that because the structures first established will direct the later ones, early experience must be important.

Finally, the ranking of children on valued traits both in and out of school sensitizes every parent of a preschool child to the fact that each will be ranked at the end of the first grade. That evaluation will influence the quality of education the child will receive from that time forward. Our commitment to a meritocratic system forces us to select candidates from the best trained, a decision made by age 10. Most parents know this sequence and from their perspective the goal is to guarantee that their child will be ahead early in the race. Because the school age child who gets off to a good start is likely, other things equal, to remain ahead, parents assume that the half-dozen years prior to school will determine that initial evaluation and interpret the profile at age 7 as a complex continuous derivative of all that has gone before.

Despite the commitment to these premises, research on both animals and infants during the last decade has implied that many qualities seen early in development may be temporary adaptations to that particular stage of growth. Fear of strangers, anxiety to separation, single-word speech, and absolute definitions of right and wrong disappear with development and may not be connected to the future characteristics that appear to be of the same substance. Perhaps they might even be omitted without altering later developmental competences.

I suspect there are some structurally preserved links across development, but also believe it is unlikely that every actor in the first scene of the play has a role in the second act. If, as cognitive psychologists have shown, the mind creates representations of events that were never experienced—prototypes created from the mental average of encounters with similar events—it is necessary to assume that the structures of mind are continually subject to change. Like the proverbial ship's planks replaced one by one until no piece of wood in the original was present in the restoration, it is possible for the 12-year-old to possess no structure that existed at age 2, even though there is overlap between the structures created a moment ago and those established a year earlier. This metaphor implies connectivity of structures over short rather than long periods. I rather like this idea because it is in some accord with evolution. Although biologists recognize a connection between all of today's living forms and ancient instances of life, most of the latter are now extinct.

On Frames of Explanation.   Description and explanation of psychological phenomena can be constructed from a subjective or an objective frame. Each is useful, each has a different function, and each has different criteria for validity. But the two frames need not be consonant. I make special mention of this point because, after 20 years of exile, self-report instruments are becoming popular once again in work on cognition, emotion, and personality. Although empirically based propositions are only one source of the state we call understanding—logic, intuition, and the testimony of others are, on occasion, valuable—statements about animals and humans written in an objective frame need not have any relation to the phenomenological perspective of the agent being described. After infancy, each person has a subjective interpretation of his or her behaviors, wishes, and experiences. From the perspective of an objective description, this private interpretation is to be regarded as an event to be understood, and not as a competing account or one to which the objective frame must accommodate. If not, there would be no need for the diagnostic categories of the psychiatrist which, most of the time, bear little relation to the patient's description or explanation of his or her symptoms.

Von Frisch's (1974) elegant descriptions of the dance of returning honeybees describe a lawful relation between the distance of the pollen source from the hive and the movement patterns of the returning bees. Von Frisch need not worry about the bees' experience. From the perspective of the person, what Wendell Garner (1981) calls the primary epistemology of the subject, perception is holistic, immediate, and unanalyzed. But the psychologist loyal to an objective epistemology analyzes into separate mechanisms what was unanalyzed by the subject.

The problem is not only that a person's linguistic description of his or her experience, whether held privately or told to another, does not contain those events that did not reach conscious awareness, but, more important, the verbal description has a unique structure—objects followed by predicates, sequencing rules that respect time and causality, and no terms for fragments of experience—that is unlikely to be faithful to the structure of the processes being summarized. Words are not finely tooled to the events they are supposed to describe. If a person exploring the interior of a deep hole with a stick is asked to describe what she is experiencing, she will talk about the shape of the hole. But the original perceptual information on which the description is based, which is not in awareness, is composed of a mosaic of pressures between the stick and the hand. Each verbal description of one's conscious experience can be likened to a pair of mechanical hands attempting to retrieve a set of small fragile forms of clumped sand whose shapes are so imperfectly matched to the mechanical hands they cannot be grasped easily. Hence, what is retrieved represents an odd fragment of what is present. Although a person's report of his experiences or thoughts has validity from the subjective frame, it may not have much validity in the objective frame.

Consider the robust phenomenon called "interference" in studies of recall memory. If we ask a subject why he cannot remember a trio of animal words after he has listened to and successfully recalled two prior sets, he is likely to say, "I can't remember." He does not feel as though anything is interfering with his ability to recall the words. Psychologists might say of the same phenomenon that there was elimination, replacement, dampening, or simply forgetting. The fruitful use of the term interference in the objective explanation is not regarded by the subject as the reason for the forgetting, and there is no reason why it should match the subjective frame.

What children and adults say to psychologists provides relevant information that we should use to gain understanding. But subjective report is often a misleading source of information for theoretical arguments written from an objective frame. Some of the current controversy in the study of human emotion derives from a desire to make the two frames concordant. Many scientists believe that the core of an emotion is contained only in the biological changes that comprise an undetected feeling tone and are revealed by face, heart, or muscle. These investigators award secondary significance to the conscious subjective evaluations that follow detection of the change in feeling tone, although they do not disregard these subsequent psychological states completely (Izard, 1977). The two states are likely to be different and should be awarded different names. The state following the smiling of a 3-month-old infant to the mother's face should not be classified with the reported state of glee that follows the realization one has passed an examination, even though the latter is accompanied by a smile.

It might be helpful to treat the distinction between disease and illness as analogous to the differences between the undetected changes in feeling tone and the evaluated changes in feeling state or, in this context, to the difference between the objective and subjective frames. Human biologists posit a set of lawful relations between specific pathogens and subsequent changes in tissues and metabolic functions. These coherences are given disease names, whether or not the patient has any conscious recognition of changes in internal function. On occasion, the individual becomes aware of the biological changes created by the disease, and if he or she evaluates them as due to a pathogenic process regards the self as having an illness. The recognition typically has non-trivial consequences, for it creates a novel psychological state that can either exacerbate or reduce the symptoms of the disease, depending upon the coping mechanisms implemented.

Each person's subjective frame is unique, limited in scope, and illuminates only part of the event to be understood. The subjective information is to be regarded as a datum with the same degree of disguise as any event, be it eye movements during sleep or a rise in heart rate to an insult. However, treating a person's subjective explanation of his or her behavior or feelings as a datum whose significance is to be discovered is quite different from regarding it on the same level as the explanation framed in the objective mode or as the criterion which the objectively written propositions must meet.

On Change and the Influence of Maturation.   Although change is characteristic of all biological events, some classes of change result in permanent reorganizations of prior structures; that is, a new set of relations among components.

Although many such changes are due only to contingent experience, observation, and reflective thought, some require the maturation of the brain. The appearance of stranger anxiety at 6 to 8 months, enhancement of retrieval memory between 8 and 12 months, and self-consciousness during the last 6 months of the second year illustrate changes that derive from maturational events in the central nervous system as long as children are growing up in environments containing people and objects.

During the last months of the first year, for example, there is an enhancement of memory that permits the universal fears of infancy to appear, and at the end of the second year children begin to display behaviors indicating that they are aware of right and wrong, aware of their competences, feeling states, and expectation to influence others. They seem to appreciate that they can control and direct their own behavior and begin to describe what they are doing. Indeed, normal children as well as deaf children learning American sign language first describe their actions with a reference to self at the same age—about 18 to 20 months (Kagan, 1981; Petitto, 1983). The suggestion that the enhancement of these and related behaviors is a consequence of brain growth finds persuasive support in data on histological changes in the young cerebral cortex (Rabinowicz, 1979).

Similarly, rhesus monkeys isolated from all contingent interactions with any living creature and raised only with inanimate objects showed maximal signs of fear in a novel environment at 4 months, the same age as monkeys raised with dogs, even though the magnitude of the reaction was muted in the isolated monkeys. It appears that the fear reaction—as evidenced by higher heart rate and distress calls—was an inevitable consequence of the maturation of the central nervous system in these isolated animals (Mason, 1978). Recitation of these findings would be of less interest if it were not for the fact that parts of developmental psychology are still under the influence of that special brand of environmentalism that grew after World War I. But having acknowledged the role of the growth of the central nervous system, our descriptions of these phenomena are still clumsy because of an old habit we find difficult to shake. The unprofitable dichotomy between the effects of biology and of experience is retained, in part, because of the statistical models we have inherited. The many investigators who use the analysis of variance and related procedures assume that the influences due to endogenous forces can be separated from the exogenous ones. Biologists have more successfully avoided the fallacy of treating complementary forces as having independent causal status. An embryo capable of cell division is formed when the sperm and egg unite; neither is the cause of the first division of the fertilized egg. In a similar vein the cognitive development of a premature infant who grows up in an economically disadvantaged home will follow a different course than a premature who grows up in an affluent home. It is not possible to determine how important prematurity or maternal acceleration is for a child's future intellectual profile. Thus, we should begin to talk of coherences rather than the partitioning of variances.

On Direction in Development.   Finally, I consider the issue of direction in growth, in contrast to change, the distinction between development and on-togenesis. I do not believe there are any special goals in human development, although humans would like to believe in such ideals. Although this skeptical premise is shared with evolutionary biologists, that is not the reason why I favor it. It is, rather, that each phase of development is characterized by both gains and losses with respect to adaptation to that period, no matter what criteria are adopted—pleasure, the meeting of standards, cognitive efficiency, empathy, love, or the capacity for moral evaluation. No one would claim that the 20-year-old's capacity for suicide is a welcome competence that the 4-year-old lacks or that the adolescent's ability to vandalize a school is preferred to the gentle innocuous play of a 2-year-old. Perhaps that is why some societies assume that childhood, like the garden of Eden, is an ideal state with growth from infancy forward being an increasingly accelerated fall from perfection.

The modern West remains committed, as it has for several centuries, to individual freedom as one of the sacred states to develop and to preserve. Locke (1693/1892) declared that "Children love liberty and therefore they should be brought to do the things that are fit for them without feeling any restraint laid upon them" (p. 83). James Sully (1896) thought the biologically best children had the most rebel in them, and that the desire to be an adult was based on the expectation that the adult role brought liberty.

Many psychologists (Erikson, 1963, is a good example) use autonomy as the translation term for freedom. But it is not intuitively obvious that freedom to act in the service of one's desires is friendlier to human nature or more conducive to social harmony—if these are the criteria chosen—than reluctantly accepting the obligation to care for a sick kin or an invitation to participate, with others, in the creation of an object of beauty. Thus, it is appropriate to ask why autonomy is often chosen by Western theorists as an end point of preference. Chinese and Japanese societies regard a love of humanity as the primary goal of development, and I am persuaded that *jen* is as reasonable a goal as autonomy. The ideals of compassion, nurture, and love place obligations on children and adults that restrict seriously each person's individual freedom.

Moral development provides a second example of a domain where an ideal terminus is assumed. Many psychologists agree with Kohlberg that there is a desirable developmental progression from fear of reprisal to a coherent principle of philosophy as the basis for adhering to a standard. Kohlberg (1981) assumes that young children inhibit acts of stealing or seizure of property because of fear of punishment. But observations reveal that 3-year-olds show signs of remorse if they cause distress to another in contexts where punishment is unlikely. A 3-year-old grabs a toy from a peer who begins to sob. After a minute or two the aggressor's facial expression changes and she generously offers the toy to the victim. It is not obvious that this act of penitence is motivated by anxiety over parental chastisement or the victim's possible retaliation. It is just as likely that the act of penance is due to the aggressor's recognition that she has violated a standard involving hurting another. Parents who discover their 4-year-old pinching himself report that the child often explains his behavior by saying that he is bad. Such a comment suggests that young children categorize the self on an evaluative dimension, and are vulnerable to displeasure if they evaluate the self as bad. It is not obvious that this phenomenon, or the inhibition of other forms of improper behavior, is based solely on a historical tie to fear of adult disapproval.

Morality remains, as it has always been, a critical human concern because people want to believe there is either a more or a less virtuous outcome in a situation of choice and insist on criteria for action. The conditions for moral virtue in modern Western society—the state that people try to attain in order to reassure themselves of their goodness—include pleasure, wealth, fame, power, autonomy, mastery, nurturance, kindness, love, honesty, work, sincerity, and belief in one's freedom. Different virtues are salient in other places. But perhaps each of these states or qualities may be traceable to some universal emotions. In brief, it is possible that beneath the extraordinary variety in surface behavior and consciously articulated virtues across time and culture, there may be a set of universal emotional states that form the basis for a limited set of moral categories that transcend locality. The human competence to experience this small set of emotional states might be likened to the preservation of basic morphological structures in evolution, each of which is expressed in varied phenotypes but descended from an original fundamental form.

Suppose that the pattern of economic, political, and social conditions within a society determines the surface virtues that will be required—whether courage, loyalty to the community, honesty, self-understanding, or a dozen other standards that dominate discussions of ethics. The surface virtues awarded the highest praise will be within the capacity of most citizens, but will require effort to attain. Assume further that the virtues easiest to promote and to defend to self are those that most effectively mute the unpleasant emotions that are provoked by violation of the standards engendered by incentives occurring with different probabilities across communities. Some potential candidates are (1) the anticipation of the varieties of anxiety that occur to the possibility of physical harm, social rejection, task failure, or feelings of anonymity; (2) feelings of empathy toward those who are in need or at risk; (3) the feeling of responsibility that follows causing harm to another; (4) feelings of fatigue and/or ennui following repeated gratifications of a desire; and (5) feelings of uncertainty that accompany encounter with discrepant events that are not easily understood or the recognition of inconsistency between thoughts or between belief and action. Because humans do not like to feel afraid, to feel sorry for someone less privileged, or to feel guilty, bored, fatigued, or confused, these unpleasant states will be classified as bad and individuals will want to replace, suppress, or avoid them. But the specific conditions that provoke these unpleasant feelings will vary with time and location and so will the specific acts that suppress them. The acts that accomplish these goals will be good and, therefore, definitive of virtue.

If the anticipation of losing a leg while defending the polis is a source of anxiety, physical courage will be a virtue. But if the incentive for anxiety is anticipated social rejection for holding an unpopular belief, loyalty to private conviction will be a celebrated virtue. Each culture in each of its historical enactments will be characterized by a unique profile of provocative conditions that tempt persons to violate local standards and a set of virtues that, if practiced, will prevent those violations, or alleviate the shame and guilt that follow them. As a result there will be different definitions of the concrete characteristics that the community encourages. It is not the relative importance of these many virtues that is an inevitable product of the human genome, but rather the capacity for empathy with another's distress and the ability to experience anxiety, shame, or guilt following the violation of standards, both of which develop in the early years.

The moral sense of children is highly canalized because of the capacity for evaluation and the competence to experience certain emotional states, but the specific ethics of a community are built from a web of social facts embedded in folk theory. Although humans do not seem to be specially programmed for a particular profile of moral missions, they are prepared to invent and believe in some ethical mission. Lagerquist had God reply to a question regarding His intention in creating human beings with, "I only intended man would never be satisfied with nothing."

EPILOGUE

Hayden White (1973) has suggested that historians typically choose one of four modes—romantic, comic, tragic, or satirical—to describe historical sequence. These modes reflect each author's evaluation of human nature as it strives to reach some goal. Each scholar also selects one of four modes of explanation— the detailing of facts, an organismic, mechanistic, or contextual interpretation. Finally, each is loyal to an ideology that reflects the attitude toward change, from conservative and liberal to radical and anarchic. Most developmental psychologists are romantic, mechanistic, and liberal, for they regard development as progressing inevitably toward a more desirable terminal state, use an explanatory mode that is mechanistic, and prefer gradual, connected change to abruptness or discontinuity. The reasons for these preferences are to be found in the deepest assumptions of our society, which historically have been optimistic, progressive, loyal to positivism, and favoring small, gradual adjustments within the political system to the disruptive effects of sudden revolution. As we continue to probe the mysteries of the growing child, we should be sensitive to the consonance between our work and these deep premises.

ACKNOWLEDGMENTS

Preparation of this paper was supported by a grant from the John D. and Catherine T. MacArthur Foundation. Some of the research summarized, in which J. Steven Reznick is a continuing collaborator, was supported by a grant from the Foundation for Child Development.

REFERENCES

Dyson, F. (1979). *Disturbing the universe.* New York: Harper & Row.

Erikson, E. H. (1963). *Childhood and society.* New York: Norton.

Garner, W. R. (1981). The analysis of unanalyzed perceptions. In M. Kubovy & J. R. Pomerantz (Eds.), *Perceptual organization* (pp. 119–139). Hillsdale, NJ: Lawrence Erlbaum Associates.

Hanson, N. R. (1961). *Patterns of discovery.* Cambridge: Cambridge University Press.

Izard, C. E. (1977). *Human emotions.* New York: Plenum.

Kagan, J. (1981). *The second year.* Cambridge: Harvard University Press.

Kagan, J., Klein, R. E., Finley, G. E., Rogoff, B., & Nolan, E. (1979). A cross-cultural study of cognitive development. *Monographs of the Society for Research in Child Development, 44*(5).

Kagan, J. & Reznick, J. S. (1984). Task involvement and cardiac response in young children. *Australian Journal Psychology 36,* 135–147.

Kagan, J., Reznick, J. S., Clarke, C., Snidman, N., & Coll, C. G. (1984). Cardiac correlates of behavioral inhibition in the young child. In M. G. H. Coles, J. R. Jennings, & J. Stern (Eds.), *Psychophysiological perspectives* (pp. 216–228). New York: Van Nostrand Reinhold.

Kohlberg, L. (1981). *The philosophy of moral development: Vol. 1. Moral stages and the idea of justice.* New York: Harper & Row.

Locke, J. (1892). *Some thoughts concerning education.* Cambridge: Cambridge University Press. (Originally published 1693).

Mason, W. A. (1978). Social experience in primate cognitive development. In G. M. Burghardt & M. Bekoff (Eds.), *The development of behavior: Comparative and evolutionary aspects* (pp. 233–251). New York: Garland Press.

Petitto, L. (1983). *From gesture to symbol.* Harvard University, Graduate School of Education.

Piaget, J. (1951). *Play, dreams, and imitation in childhood* (C. Gattegno & F. M. Hodgson, trans.). London: Routledge & Kegan Paul.

Rabinowicz, T. (1979). The differentiate maturation of the human cerebral cortex. In F. Falkner & J. M. Tanner (Eds.), *Human growth* (Vol. 3, pp. 97–123). New York: Plenum.

Russell, B. (1912). *The problems of philosophy.* Oxford: Clarendon Press.

Starkey, D. (1983). Familiar and unfamiliar virtual objects: A study of intersensory coordination in infancy (Doctoral dissertation, Brandeis University, 1983). *Dissertation Abstracts International, 44B,* 128.

Sully, J. (1896). *Studies of childhood.* New York: D. Appleton.

Thorndike, E. L. (1905). *The elements of psychology.* New York: A. G. Seiler.

Von Frisch, K. (1974). Decoding the languages of the bee. *Science, 185,* 663–668.

White, H. (1973). *Metahistory: The historical imagination in nineteenth-century Europe.* Baltimore: Johns Hopkins University Press.

DISCUSSION

GILLIGAN: Jerry, the perspective of an objective description: Whose?

KAGAN: The objective frame is the frame of the group who call themselves empiricists. Their's is the object description. That band of weary travelers tries to understand phenomena in an objective mode.

GILLIGAN: So there's an agreement, then, among the group.

KAGAN: There is always an attempt toward or striving for consensus.

BRUNER: I'm glad that there are still some epistemological optimists around. Jerry, you were very honest. You stated your claim, and you denied psychological abstractions and continuity and insisted on specificity and data-driveness. Having done that, which was a splendid start, you let yourself fall into the trap of buying evolutionary biology, lock, stock and barrel, as a basis for continuities. You have stated what is implicitly, and this is okay (I happen not to agree with it), an anti-historical, an anti-cultural view. You talk about four universal drives which plainly grow out of an evolutionary biology perspective as bases for universal ways of defining the virtuous versus the non-virtuous, so that all that history can do, or that a culture can do, is to find realization rules, ways of expressing these.

One faces, it seems to me, a choice here. The choice is, on the one hand, to say this loses sight of the fact that the realities are to some very important degree created by language. The language may indeed have a biological base but somehow, as Peter Medewar has put it, the one thing that characterizes the emergence of human language and the human symbolic system is to lead to a discontinuity with evolutionary Darwinian type of biology and lead us eventually to a Lamarckian point of view. As one looks at human culture one has to view the extent to which the human tool kit of concepts and so forth are better described as the passing on of acquired characteristics. One can take the view that these two should dispute each other. We dispute these things and we'll go on disputing them doubtless until our last breath. I think it's rich.

On the other hand there is another view, driven to some extent by pluralism, that it is marvelous that there are epistemological optimists who pursue this line, which is very worried about our tendency to make errors in psychology because we do not have a connected set of principles from which to derive things. Pursue it, but let us also pursue another line which is so different as to be incommensurable, that grows out of a kind of contemporary anthropology and what I want to call, for short, anthropological psychology, which takes as its premise that the main thing about man is that he has a language which creates reality. He sets up symbol systems for which he dies, often in a fashion which maximizes his anxiety, which sometimes violates what might be his empathy, which permits him to experience stretches of boredom which are beyond belief. One of the examples—war—is notable for the fact that a few experience terror, but most who live in it experience boredom. And as for uncertainty, why then do we create the Hong Kong stock exchange? Now I prefer to follow the pluralistic line. I want to say that two good things are better than one. If one can make a good thing out of a developmental psychology that takes its hints from evolutionary biology, an interesting and powerful field, great! At the same time, it seems to me that issues that come out of the more anthropological psychology, that take meaning, culture, and their negotiation as central, is another kind of thing.

Some people now say, "It's so awful. What is the state of the field of human development that we have these two very different kinds of things?" In some way I think it's very lively, partly by virtue of the fact that these are two fields.

I don't think that I would want to go into the game of giving you instances in which those four things, or in which the other seven, are violated by specific cultural situations because I think that each one would have the interesting effect of sharpening up your evolutionary biology perspective, which would be good. We will doubtless do this over the next years, but, if you do it by evolutionary biological conceptions, don't let yourself be satisfied by those four points because they are going to get you into the same trouble that the law of effect got learning theory into. It got it into a box in which it had to define things as anticipation of anxiety, which were so far removed from what one would ordinarily call anticipation anxiety. So, I feel vaguely as if this were the House of Commons and I was speaking as the loyal opposition, but I don't really think that one would want to compromise between them. I think that each should go in their own direction without compromise.

KAGAN: I agree. But if one has a choice, should one dwell on the remarkable differences in human beings across time and culture, or should one try to look for the similarities? My talk emphasized the similarities, but does not deny the enormous diversity.

KAPLAN: I'm going to deal with only one aspect of the first part of your paper for a moment. I may read you incorrectly, but I think you were an advocate of Blake's aphorism: "To generalize is to be an idiot, individuality is the alone distinction of merit."

KAGAN: Not bad.

KAPLAN: Because, as I understand it, what you were looking for was the formulation of the form if A and B and C and D and E and F, and so on, then X. On the other hand, you recognized also that A and B and C become A

prime, and double prime, and triple prime. So ultimately what you are looking for as a goal and what you took to be objective science is a statement of all
of the variables which would predict or be causally related to a specific
variable, having a telephone book series of all the items and always looking
for greater and greater particularity. Did I understand you correctly? And that
you take to be the aim of science.

KAGAN: One aim, yes.

KAPLAN: Oh, I just wanted to make sure that I understood you correctly.

KAGAN: Bernie understood me exactly. [Laughter]

WARTOFSKY: I don't have any questions. I just want to attack you. [Laughter]
The biological basis of ethics is a very, very old game. It goes back at least to
the 19th century, probably to the 18th. It has been played out again most
recently in Wilson's work on sociobiology. Wilson's rather crude version of it
in the earlier works, and his more sophisticated version of the same thing in
the later work was qualified in part by Mary Midgley, the English philosopher
who wrote a book called *Beast and Man* and tried to clean up Wilson's act.
Primarily, Midgley, a student of Iris Murdoch, has a good background in
ethics and made the argument that Wilson was all wrong in reducing ethics
and culture to biology in the early work. What we have to understand instead,
she argues, is that all biology does is to set the constraints on what *kinds* of
ethical developments can take place; and these are themselves developments
on a relatively plastic base of a few biological types. I don't remember how
many she had. . . . You have four "basic drives."

KAGAN: They were meant to be only suggestive and not exhaustive.

WARTOFSKY: Yes, but I think her argument (which I have criticized in a
review) and yours suffer from the same defect as Wilson's does. It might be
heuristically interesting to see how far we can get in tracing traits to genes, or
ethics to emotional primitives. On the other hand, [there] doesn't seem to be
any particular warrant or argument for doing so. William James had a theory
of emotion which wasn't too far from this, tracing it in a kind of evolutionary
way. In the *Psychology,* he talked about the origins of our emotional expressions, e.g., expressing anger by gritting one's teeth, which James traced
back to what dogs do when they are threatening to bite you; therefore, he saw
in the animal behavior the sources of human emotional expression. Darwin
had a lovely essay on the expression of emotion in animals and man. But to
take this to the point of making it the basis for a mapping of the virtues seems
to be wrong. Now, what you are giving us is a kind of up-dated biological
version of the 18th-century theory of moral sentiments. I don't know whether
that's what you were talking about when you referred to Hume, or Hutcheson,
or the others.

KAGAN: Yes, I would say that's fair.

WARTOFSKY: The notion that we have innate moral sensibilities—e.g., sympathy, in Hume—was *not* taken by the moral sentiment theorists as a biological argument, although it *was* taken as an essentialist argument. It's part of human nature to have these sentiments, they held, and then these basic sentiments vary by custom and history and circumstance. But the move to biology seems to me to be a very, very strong one, much stronger than Jerome Bruner described it. I think he was being a pluralistic, liberal, Habermasian, communicative discourse type.

KAGAN: Marx, all you're saying so far is that you're disagreeing. Now you have to give some evidence.

WARTOFSKY: I don't have to give evidence yet. All that I have to do is show where I think there is weakness in the argument. What you said was that when people give reasons for why they do certain things we can explain it by means of some description in objective terms which needn't have anything to do with the phenomenological self-description or self-understanding.

KAGAN: Right.

WARTOFSKY: And then I'm not clear whether you mean that we are introducing a theoretical term which we use as an intervening variable in order to explain what we phenomenologically or ordinarily regard as forgetting— using interference here. Where does that get you? In other words, are you alleging, given the realist beginning of the paper, that there is such a thing as interference which takes place or that this is a convenient theoretical fiction?

KAGAN: The latter.

WARTOFSKY: Therefore, if that's what it is, all it does is correlate data. It's an intervening variable. It makes no allegation concerning what the bees are doing.

KAGAN: Absolutely not.

WARTOFSKY: But then you spoke of changes in feeling tone.

KAGAN: That's right.

WARTOFSKY: Now, unless I misunderstand the term feeling tone, I take that to be a phenomenological description.

KAGAN: No. I said that I'm using the term feeling tone in an objective frame. I am assuming that there are changes that occur in the biological states of human beings that go undetected. Those changes I call feeling tones.

WARTOFSKY: That are undetected by . . .

KAGAN: . . . by conscious awareness of the agent I'm describing.

BRUNER: You should watch your language though. That's a funny way to talk about . . .

KAPLAN: . . . feeling tones.

KAGAN: Changes in tone if you prefer.

WARTOFSKY: Okay. I'll buy "tone," since we use "tonus" as a good kinesthetic term. It seems to me, though, that if that's the kind of description you want, then reports on sequences of such bodily changes or changes of tone are not yet a report on the process that's going on, which is of an intentional sort. I don't want to get into the argument on reasons and causes, but I think you're vulnerable there. Again, I'm pointing out where I think there is a difficulty.

You made the point that neural capacities for self-reference occur independently in deaf-mutes and in those who learn language in another way, and this leads you to jump, again, to a biological characterization . . .

KAGAN: Participation of the growth of the brain, right.

WARTOFSKY: Right, neural capacity for self-reference in the central nervous system. Again, I don't see why that jump is at all warranted since both the deaf-mute and the speaking children are speaking a language and being socialized in what is, after all, a common culture, whether in sign language or in verbal speech, and it doesn't seem to me that the jump to neural capacities as an explanation for the simultaneity of the development is at all necessary here. There are lots of other variables of a cultural or social sort that could easily be plugged in. Now that's not an argument to demolish your argument. I'm agreeing with you in the sense that you say, "Okay, let's look at that," but I would not proceed from such a consideration to your conclusions.

Finally, whatever neural or neurosomatic developments there may be certainly would provide, under certain circumstances which could be specified, the *necessary* conditions for the development of social, linguistic, intentional, and other sorts of activity, but *no more* than necessary conditions, because it is possible for these conditions to be present and for the event not to take place. It's also, I think, difficult to establish what the mapping would be on neural development. For example, one could say that 1-year-olds can't do arithmetic and 6-year-olds in general can, maybe even cross-culturally if you give them the proper schooling, and that therefore at 5 there is a development of the neural connection which makes arithmetic possible. That seems to me to be a completely gratuitous step.

KAGAN: Marx, it seems to me you are saying politely to me, "I disagree," and I respect your will on this issue. But you have no facts to contravert...

WARTOFSKY: I don't see that anything of what you claim follows from what you...

KAGAN: Whenever one can demonstrate temporal concordances for some characteristics of human children across time and culture, where one knows that there are differences in experiential context, one is using a method of indirect proof. That's all we can do. I regard as more persuasive than you do the fact that when one looks at children from varied cultures, signs of a moral sense emerge at about the same time. Read Preyer, Sully, and so many diarists of the 18th and 19th century. All show a remarkable concordance. Somewhere between 18 and 24 months children begin to say things like "yuckie," "fix doll," "bad," "good." Why? Why do Pettito's deaf children and our own children begin to refer to self within 6 weeks of one another? One can say that the children had similar experiences. But I am impressed by the concordance and use it to argue that there probably is something important maturing in the central nervous system. That's the argument. It's not an original argument, but it is not weakened by the fact that you don't find it agreeable.

WARTOFSKY: No, it's not that I find it disagreeable. I think there are many other reasons one could give for this concordance.

KAGAN: Absolutely, but it seems to me that the burden of proof is as much on you as it is on me.

WARTOFSKY: Okay.

BRUNER: But part of the burden of proof on you is also to explain the discordances, Jerry, which you would have to do.

KAPLAN: I'm going to continue if I may for a moment. Do you agree to how I formulated your position before? [Laughter] It seems to me that if you carry that to the extreme, any general term or any supposed concordances between classes of events, you are saying, always hides the distinctiveness of each of the members of the class, and a precise statement should lead to a Leibnizian conclusion that all of the predicates are contained in the subject. Any kind of statement that this is related to that, you say, really hides the fact that if you look more closely you will always find that the individual members are different. You have no ground for saying "whenever," or "if then," using general terms. It will always be a specific, almost biographical statement of that individual. You say that science—you notice I'm not criticizing, I'm just asking [Laughter]—that science for you then constitutes an infinite series of statements about individual episodes. I will not take that that is not possible (obviously it's not possible to get that infinite statement), but I just want to make sure again that I've understood you correctly.

KAGAN: But now let me add one caveat. At any point we can stop with approximate propositions that share relatedness knowing that there is error in that proposition. It is a standard stochastic statement about...

KAPLAN: If you know that it's error you have to be able to think the other side of the error.

KAGAN: Right.

KAPLAN: So you know at least vaguely what it would be.

KAGAN: You have an ideal toward which you are moving. One can have classes of events and know there is an error in the proposition. It seems to me that's the fundamental tenet of empirical science. You can say that the tenet is flawed.

KAPLAN: But one step further, if I may. You don't have "if-then" statements then; you have "thus far, whenever"—tomorrow it may change. So you have a series of actuarial statements for the moment.

KAGAN: Exactly.

KAPLAN: Okay. I just wanted to be sure I understand what you said.

BERNSTEIN: I'm wondering if I heard the same paper as my colleagues because Bruner and Wartofsky interpret you as manqué biologist, and I didn't hear that at all, so I would like to find out whether I'm confused, they're confused, or you're confused.

WARTOFSKY: You weren't listening carefully, Richard. [Laughter]

BERNSTEIN: Let me just develop the logic of it. There is something that you enunciated that everybody would agree to: that one cannot forget that we are biological creatures, that any theory of psychological development has to take that into account, and that poses certain kinds of constraints. Nobody disagrees with that.

KAGAN: I thought Marx did.

BERNSTEIN: I don't believe he would disagree with that statement as I put it. The thing is, where you go next: your critique of exaggerated or abstracted notions of competence, your own insistence on the importance of discontinuity, that things could really change. It seems to me that you are opening up a tremendous gap between what can be interpreted as psychological development and any kinds of biological constraints. You put it in terms of different codes and moralities. I thought that you were making not only a tentative but a very minimalistic claim about morality, and that is that one can note something like our distinctions—good, bad, virtue, vice—across cultures. Over and above that, it seems to me you were sheerly speculative here because you weren't giving any kind of evidence. It may be that there are primitive kinds of universal emotions. You were not yet affirming that, but certainly any connection between that and specific morality is something that was left open and indeterminate.

KAGAN: Richard, you said it more elegantly; that's exactly what I intended to say.

BERNSTEIN: Well, if that's what you intended it seems to me that Bruner and Wartofsky misread you.

KAGAN: Jerry, maybe you want...

BRUNER: I do have one thing to say. If you tell me that there is a set of atomic propositions to which all complex propositions can be reduced, then what I'm with is essentially the point of view that was very prevalent, in Urmson's account of this. When you start telling me that there are logical primitives and that things can be reduced to it, then it seems to me that you are making a very, very strong claim.

KAGAN: But that's not what I'm saying.

BRUNER: But I think you said that there is no culture in which you will find forms of valuation that are not somehow reducible to a set of atomic propositions. It seemed to me it was a reductionism to a set of universals about preference for one state over another. And if you didn't mean that, I shall be very happy because I don't like that point of view.

KAGAN: I am declaring that there is a universal avoidance reaction to displeasure and an appetitive one for pleasure.

BRUNER: That I will grant, but what has that to do with the reducibility of culture and cultural values?

KAGAN: I intended to say, and Richard said it well, that biology prepares the 3-year-old for a moral sense, which is given form by experience, history, and culture.

GILLIGAN: I was fascinated by your identifying the capacity for empathy with another's distress and the capacity to experience anxiety on the violation of standards as the two foundations of the moral sense—precisely the two moral forces I've described. Looking for origins, I connect these to different dimensions of relationships, claiming these are universally present in young children's experience. I don't see how they connect to innate emotions. How do you come up with these two?

KAGAN: It seems to me, Marx may not like this, that if one examines relevant essays—Plato, Aristotle, Geach—their a priori views as to the human virtues always show concern for people at risk.

GILLIGAN: No. I agree with you that these occur, that these can be observed in old accounts of children you see about the same age. I am not clear where you derive these from.

KAGAN: The capacity for empathy is inherent in children. A person might lose it with development, for it leads to an unpleasant state one does not like to experience chronically. The feeling state is a basic capacity that provokes the community to invent a virtue like charity...

GILLIGAN: Inherent in children—you mean...

KAGAN: I intend the meaning of preparedness. Biologists say finch are prepared to learn the song of their species if they hear for a short time a recording of the song of their species. I say children are prepared to be empathetic in that sense.

GILLIGAN: That's interesting because then you have to talk about the context in which the capacity emerges.

KAGAN: Human beings.

GILLIGAN: Relationships?

KAGAN: Right.

BRUNER: Although I have attacked the concept of competence when I was wearing my linguistic hat, I do want to set one thing right. I think that there you were unfair. The concept of competence is based on a single instance which says, in effect, therefore there must be a competence. It says then if you find the right conditions, performance will conform to or deviate systematically from competence, depending upon those other conditions. Rather than competence being restricted in that sense, it is essentially a kind of permission to assume that if there was one performance, there are conditions that will produce similar performances. So you shouldn't be quite so harsh.

KAGAN: But what's the name of the competence, Jerry? What do you want to name that competence?

BRUNER: The competence is simply called things like "competence for empathy," "competence for avoidance of anxiety," and so forth. Curiously enough, you were using those terms in exactly the same way as Noam [Chomsky] uses competence as competence for language as a whole. He never talks about competence for, for example, possessives, or competence for using the copula, etc.

KAGAN: That's fair.

AUDIENCE MEMBER: It doesn't seem to me you're heeding your own warning not to think in terms of the either-or, biological or environmental, aspects.

Why do you focus for an explanation of these kinds of concordances on biological readiness?

KAGAN: Only because each statement is always a reaction to what the popular belief was in the past. Without the period from World War I to the 1960s, you would be yawning, and I probably wouldn't have said what I did. As you know, since World War I, American psychologists have declared you've got to teach children morality. We use the term *psychopath,* referring to a person who never learned a moral sense. But one can only lose a moral sense.

AUDIENCE MEMBER: I can't get from your extreme epistemological particularism, which says thou shalt not generalize beyond particular conditions of this experiment to any other conditions whatsoever, to your ability to then set up categorical comparisons between a developmental sequence here and a developmental sequence over here. I don't mind the latter too much, but I can't reconcile it with the former.

KAGAN: That's a fair criticism, and it's related to Jerry's recent comment. I plead guilty to that. I have not been honest to the first part of the paper, but I believe the first part of the paper and had a moral fall in the latter part.

WARTOFSKY: There is an anecdote one might choose from Kierkegaard, because he too had the view that culture really developed from boredom (a rather remarkable passage in the *Concluding Unscientific Postscript*). He writes: God was bored, so he created Adam. Then they were bored together. So God created Eve, and then they were...

GILLIGAN: Never bored again.

WARTOFSKY: No, and then they were bored together, and so they produced Cain and Abel, and then they were bored *en famille,* and he goes on, and on, and finally he ends up with the final culmination of this history of boredom as exemplified in the Danish postal service. [Laughter]

5 Value Presuppositions in Theories of Human Development

Bernard Kaplan
Clark University and
Heinz Werner Institute for Developmental Psychology

Although professionals may protest, I submit that we are all "developmental psychologists" just as we are all "philosophers." With regard to the latter—that we are "philosophers"—surely, we all have conceptions as to the way things are (let us call this ontology); convictions about acceptable ways of arriving at knowledge (let us call this epistemology); beliefs about how human beings ought to behave or act with respect to fellow human beings and with regard to infra-human beings (let us call this ethics); convictions about the legitimacy or illegitimacy of various inferences (let us call this logic). Professional philosophers may regard our conceptions as vague, inconsistent, diffuse, irrational, and so on. In so doing, they presumably think that there is a better, more adequate, more mature, more advanced, more fully developed way of arriving at what there is, of what claims are knowledge-worthy, of how a human being ought to conduct his or her life in relation to other human beings and even to infra-human beings. Moreover, in much of their teaching and writing, they will intimate that their way is a better way, a more advanced way, a more highly developed way. They will seek to induce *not merely a change but a developmental advance* in their colleagues and students.

With regard to the former—"that we are all developmental psychologists"— it is obvious that we all have conceptions of how different human beings change in different ways over the life span. We also have conceptions as to why they change in the way they do. We also entertain beliefs about what human beings should be doing (or be capable of doing) at different periods during the life span, and we may become unsettled or disturbed, especially if those human beings are ourselves or kin to us, if what we believe ought to be done is not done. Once again, we usually have (however ill-formed or inchoate) hypotheses as to why the human beings in question do not or can not do what we believe they ought to do or be capable of doing.

Professional students of human development may regard our conceptions as vague, inconsistent, diffuse, irrational, and so on. They may even in a moment of "forgetfulness" characterize them by that tabooed term *primitive*. They may then seek to provide us with a better, more adequate, more mature, more fully developed account of how human beings change over the life span and why they change as they do.[1] Thus professional "developmental psychologists," in much of their teaching and writing, will intimate that their way is a better way, a more advanced way, a more developed way. They will again seek to induce in their colleagues and students not merely an alternative or different way of thinking about human development, *but a developmentally more advanced* way. One might say, a more valuable or worthwhile way. And although they may make a show of pure tolerance or indifference with regard to alternative ways of construing human development, in their heart of hearts they are likely to hold that their way of construing human development, describing human development, and explaining human development—either in whole or with respect to selected aspects—is a more advanced way of going about the enterprise.

Parenthetically, I might add that some developmental psychologists with an addiction to a REALIST ontology, an epistemological conviction that science (narrowly conceived) is the sole or preeminent way to discover the nature of a self-subsistent (noumenal) Reality, and a firm belief that values are a matter of taste or cultural convention will maintain that their way of arriving at a knowledge of the structure of Reality is developmentally more advanced than the ways (e.g., intuition) of others. Developmentally more advanced, *simpliciter*; and not on the basis of idiosyncratic preference or cultural custom. Developmentally more advanced not only for themselves or the "small coterie of emancipated souls" (Dewey) to which they belong, but for anyone and everyone. Moreover, they will often take the quest for a knowledge of Reality and Truth as a mandatory value (to use J.N. Findlay's phrase)—something that all human beings ought to pursue. To the extent that human beings or groups of human beings prefer "ignorance" to "knowledge" or "delusions" to "facts," they will be taken to be less than fully developed human beings.

And even if, to avoid inconsistency and charges of "elitism," they opt for cultural and ultimately, individual sovereignty in matters of what is True, what is Good, what is Beautiful, they are likely to regard their posture of pure tolerance,

---

[1]Some may even claim to have a theory, or the beginnings of a theory, composed of principles, laws and empirical generalizations, in terms of which they can or will be able to predict how a human being changes, given certain specified conditions. The attainment of such a theory is taken by them as the Telos of a theory of human development—a value to be quested after. Whether this ought to be the aim of a theory of human development is arguable. In any case theories of that kind—the natural science sense of theory—constitute a null class with regard to human development and are likely to have an application, if they did exist, only in strongly totalitarian societies (See Mills, 1959).

and the acceptance of whatever values people or societies entertain, as a developmentally more advanced approach to human development than any adopted by others who reject—as values, not as "facts"—such cultural, cognitive, and moral relativism.

I have called attention to these phenomena about ourselves in our typical everyday existences[2] as a point of departure for discussing the general topic of this symposium: value presuppositions in theories of human development. In everyday life, we do not as a rule take human development—or, better, the development of the human beings that we are concerned about—to be merely or mainly changes that take place over time. We are concerned with whether they achieve certain ends or manifest certain achievements at a proper time, for example, achievements in speech, achievements in locomotion, achievements in getting along with others in roughly specified ways. We realize that some of these achievements may take time, and we are usually tolerant, and even indulgent, up to a certain point, if the desiderated performance—let us call such ideal performances in any domain *teloi*—is not realized. Beyond that point, however, we may become concerned and even distressed, and look for the "causes" for the "failure" or "defect." With regard to some of the teloi, we take them to be in the nature of the beast—as if the individual were naturally, and without either prompting or consciousness, directed toward their accomplishment. We might try to facilitate the process by various kinds of assistance, but we expect it to take place, culminating in the telos, more or less automatically. With regard to other teloi, we take them to be, so to speak, antagonistic to the nature of the beast; something that the beast must learn or take over from us or from others, if the individual is to become fully human, fully mature. Failure to take over these teloi, and to make them operative in one's life at proper times, is taken as a "defect" or "failure"; and attempts are made to determine the "causes" of such defects or failure and to provide remedies or therapeutic treatment in the broadest sense so that the individual will get back on, or get on, "the right track." These teloi are often called "values," and we hope that such values will be adopted by, and become inculcated in, the growing human being. The failure to take over certain values and to operate in terms of them in one's life and in one's relation to others is tantamount to being less than fully human.

Now, admittedly, the teloi we take for granted in the nature of the beast, and the values we take as mandatory for individuals to adopt and operate in terms of if they are to be fully human, are human inventions, and in many, perhaps all instances, sociocultural inventions. We may take the "categorical imperative" or some version of operating "rationally" in one's existence as mandatory values—even if they are only sporadically attained or never fully established. In other sociocultural entities in space and time studied by anthropologists and

---

[2]For further discussion, see my paper, "Genetic-dramatism: old wine in new bottles (in Wapner & Kaplan, 1983). For an illuminating discussion of the concept of human existence see Wild (1966).

historians, there may be different values; a different ordering of values, in terms of degree of importance; values *toto coelo* opposed to ours. What we take as values to be adopted and striven for, they take as disvalues to be blocked or stamped out and vice versa. What we take as criteria for the fully developed human being, they reject, and what they take as criteria, we reject. In other words, different sociocultural groups may have different notions as to what constitutes ideal human development. They may also have different notions as to the "causes" that promote or preclude whatever they take to be ideal human development. And, finally, they may have different notions as to what has to be done to get individuals on the right track with regard to the approximation or attainment of ideal human development. In sum, in a certain broad sense of theory, they will have different theories about what constitutes the field of human development, what are the causes or occasions for the attainment or failure to attain certain teloi and values[3] that are taken as constitutive of full human development, and what remedies, devices, or means should be used to overcome blockage of the movement toward full human development. Would we say in such instances that there are values ingredient in their theories (and our everyday theories) of human development (Kaplan, 1983a)?

Thus far, it would seem that what constitutes human development is dependent on culture, and different cultures may have different conceptions (theories) about human development. Max Weber remarked on one occasion that "the concept of culture is a value-concept." "Empirical reality," he maintained, "becomes 'culture' to us because and insofar as we relate it to value ideas. It includes those segments and only those segments of reality which have become significant to us because of this value relevance. Only a small portion of existing concrete reality is colored by our value-conditioned interest and it alone is significant to us. It is significant because it reveals relationships which are important to us due to their connection with our values" (Weber, 1977, p. 27). Now, if human development is a culture concept (Cassirer, 1961), is it too a value concept—a value concept wherever it occurs? A value concept whether it is maintained by an anonymous group or articulated by a solitary, albeit socioculturally conditioned, individual—a Hegel, a Marx, a Freud, a Jung, a Piaget, a Werner? Do the theories—I would prefer to call them approaches or perspectives—of these giants, with regard to human development, transcend cultural parochialism and the putative relativism of cultures and values? Or, are their theories and ours, if we proffer them, inevitably culture-bound and riven with local values that some, perhaps many, of us would regard merely as a matter of taste?

---

[3]Although distinctions may be drawn, and perhaps ought to be drawn, between teloi and values in certain contexts, they will often be used interchangeably unless specifically noted. The terms *telos* and *teloi* are often used synecdochically to stand for ends, goals, values, and so on.

Allow me to dilate on this point for a moment. The "object," human development, that occupies the attention of many of us here and elsewhere, does not seem to be an object or process in nature, like a rock or a hurricane, putatively existing or occurring, irrespective of and independent of human existence or human interest; it is, rather, constituted by human beings for human beings, and seemingly differently constituted by different groups of human beings. Nonanimate and perhaps nonhuman nature has no need of ends, purposes, or values. It is human beings who introduce teloi and values and construe development in terms of such teloi and values. It is in terms of them that one brings to the fore relevant fields for developments of various kinds. They determine, in large measure, which of the myriad actions and patterns of action[4] manifested in the lives of human beings during the course of their lives are pertinent to any specified developmental sequence (motor, linguistic, cognitive) or to human development as a whole. It is in terms of them that it makes sense to speak of development at all (as distinct from change). It is with regard to them, and their expected or hoped for progressive approximation or realization during certain phases of an individual's life, that we take individuals to be retarded, arrested, normal, pathological, and so forth. It is with regard to them, and the modes of operation that are taken to constitute their full actualization, that we consider performances and patterns of performance to be relatively primitive or relatively advanced.

Now if teloi are "culture relative" or "culture bound," and claims about the development of some aspect of human functioning or human functioning itself depends on the teloi, then it makes no sense to speak of development *tout court* or to assume a priori that human development is everywhere the same. Any change in the telos, or the order of value of the teloi, will entail different developmental sequences and different interpretations and evaluations of what human beings are doing (Watkins, 1982).

It is important to mention—and perhaps this is as good a place as any—that in many societies human development is not a happening or a process that is automatically instantiated by diverse human beings as a matter of nature. Human development is rather a desideratum, a value to be struggled for and achieved. Ironically, perhaps, for Wernerians, an achievement rather than a process— although, to be sure the meanings of these terms here are different from those the terms were given in Werner's classic paper (Werner, 1937). One has not fully developed until one has realized that achievement. In that sense one may never fully develop, at least in what we ordinarily call a lifetime. When Pico della Mirandola talks about possibilities of human beings in his Oration on the Dignity

---

[4]It is imperative as Kenneth Burke (1945) among others has pointed out to distinguish between action and motion. Actions, some of which can occur in the absence of motion, are characteristically culturally defined.

of Man, when Feuerbach speaks of God as man's alienated essence, when Marx (Karl but probably Wartofsky too) and Ortega y Gasset insist that human beings have no fixed nature but are transformed in the course of human history, when Lancelot Law Whyte talks of "the next development of man" and P.D. Ouspensky of "the psychology of man's possible evolution," they are all alluding, it seems to me, to the "fact" that human development is not fixed, not merely an object for inquiry, description, and explanation, but something to be struggled for. It is hopefully clear from all this that how one characterizes "human development" is intimately connected not only with one's value presuppositions, but with one's ontological and epistemological prejudices. And of course with one's conception of the relation between theory and praxis.

You will perhaps see from all of this why I maintain that there is no reason to believe that progressive approximations to certain locally, or even generally, valued modes of operation or ways-of-being-in-the-world are inherent either in the historical process or in the biographical or ontogenetic process. During the 19th century, and even earlier, it was widely believed that the historical process and the evolutionary process were intrinsically "orthogenetic"—that is, were governed by some immanent law leading ineluctably to rationality, freedom, perfection, or some other ultimate telos.[5] It is still with us in many so-called stage theories either in history or ontogenesis, in which a necessary and inevitable sequence of stages is posited. I do not believe that there is any warrant for the postulation of immanent laws in history or ontogenesis (see Popper's *Poverty of Historicism,* 1957), although I can see the value of positing such a series as an "ideal of natural order" (Toulmin)—a developmental order—in order to assess what takes place in the course of time. Time, then, is not necessarily the Mother of Perfection, and even if it were, Perfection (or the attainment of freedom, emancipation, etc.) is not a parthenogenic offspring. If one characterizes "development" as I do, following Goethe and Werner, as a movement toward perfection, then the passage of time—either on the culture-historical level or on the level of the individual human being—does not ensure "development." Even if one accepts as fact that the conception of "ideal human development" varies for different social groups, I would wager that at least with respect to many, and characteristically the most distinctive and important teloi, it is something to be worked for in order to be attained. It is not something that emerges as a matter of course in the nature of getting older. "Older," as more than one person has remarked, "is not necessarily wiser."

---

[5]See Löwith (1949), Kaplan (1983d), Berlin (1954). The belief was subsequently applied to human ontogenesis via the Meckel-Haeckel "biogenetic law" or "law of recapitulation" (see Russell, 1916/1982).

Now, if I am correct in what I have said thus far, one will not be able to discover anything about human development if one accepts the dogma of immaculate perception, if one merely records the "facts" of ontogenesis and examines solely the causes of their coming to be and passing away. Development is only rendered "visible," so to speak, if one adopts a developmental perspective. Such a perspective, I submit, involves the presumption of teloi, an ordering of teloi, and an ordering of the means or modes of operation for realizing the teloi. From such a perspective, development pertains to progressions of forms with respect to functions or means with respect to ends. This order is logically independent of the temporal or chronological order—and may be characterized as relatively more primitive and more advanced modes of approaching or approximating teloi. The order is also logically independent of so-called causes or mechanisms of changes or transformations. One can construct, and has constructed, developmental sequences of modi operandi with respect to certain teloi, without the slightest idea of the necessary, sufficient, or necessary and sufficient conditions, for the coming into being or passing away of either more primitive or more advanced modes—that is, without knowing the "whys" of the "whats." In a full-scale developmental approach to the phenomena of human ontogenesis, where one is concerned with interventions to promote development or to overcome obstacles to it, means-ends analysis and causal analysis are both required, but one should recognize that though complementary, they are distinct (Cassirer, 1961).

As I reflect back on the things I have said thus far, I realize that I have been elliptical in many places, and that I may have advanced claims and proposals that seem incompatible and may even be incompatible with each other. For those to whom consistency is a mandatory value, incumbent on all, my performance would then be, and ought to be, taken as relatively primitive. Of course, for those to whom "consistency is the hobgoblin of small minds" the developmental status of my modus operandi would be different. One issue we shall have to discuss is whether we should leave it at that—groups, and ultimately individuals granted the sovereignty to determine their own teloi or values, that is, cultural and ultimately individual relativism not as fact but as value. Or whether there is some way beyond Thrasymachus—justice is the interest of the stronger—as to what values ought to be the highest ones to strive for in becoming fully human wherever one rests one's head. We now reject the thesis that whatever individuals take to be their values ought to be their values—a version of whatever is, is right. Shall we accept the thesis that whatever cultural or subcultural groups take to be their ultimate values—especially with regard to so-called moral and ethical issues—ought to be uncritically taken as such? Individual as God. Society as God. I hope I have time to come back to this issue, at least, before I close.

Before I turn to that issue, however, I would like to iterate my view of "developmental psychology" more concisely and directly, since it may have come out only obliquely in what I have thus far said. In stating my view here I acknowledge that form of plagiarism that Marcel Proust took to be the worst kind: plagiarism from one's self.[6] I unblushingly admit to some tinkering.

I start with the question, "What is developmental psychology?" Lurking beneath this seemingly simple and innocuous question is a serpentine ambiguity. Developmental psychology can be defined in terms of what self-proclaimed or officially canonized developmental psychologists do, or in terms of what one thinks they ought to be doing. The issue here is analogous to questions such as "What is justice?" "What is art?" "What is value?" "What is science?" Although such questions, on the surface, seem to ask for straightforward descriptions, it almost inevitably turns out that the answers are "persuasive definitions" (Stevenson, 1944). And those who define in terms of the "mainstream"—for example, the operationalists who hold that "developmental psychology" is what developmental psychologists do—are as much engaged in persuasive definition (maintaining the status quo) as those who suggest a radically different definition of the enterprise.

It should be obvious, as Max Black (1954) pointed out some years ago in his paper on "The definition of scientific method," that persuasive definitions are not regulated simply or mainly by "what is the case." They are advanced in terms of certain interests, and therefore reflect ethical and axiological considerations as well as logical and methodological ones. Inevitably, they are political and ideological, even though they may be presented as neutral and dispassionate. I suggested this point before in discussing the concept of "human development."

Now, my definition of "developmental psychology." *Developmental psychology is a practico-theoretical discipline, a policy discipline, concerned with the perfection (including liberation or freedom) of the individual and the perfection of those modes of operation promoting the perfection of the individual.* Its aim is to facilitate—and here I use many of the terms that are often deprecated by academic developmentalists—the self-actualization, freedom from bondage, individuation, and so forth of human beings. To do so, it undertakes inquiries into the variety of factors, operative at particular times and places, that facilitate or impede progress toward the goal and suggests policies and practices to institute the facilitative factors and eliminate those factors that interfere with optimal development. It should be obvious, in terms of this definition of the field, that *human development* itself is not defined by observations, systematic or otherwise, of what actually occurs in childhood, over the life span, and so on. To use Northrop's (1947) formulation, "development" is a *concept by postulation,* not a *concept by intuition.* It pertains to a rarely, if ever, attained ideal, not to the actual. We do not discover the nature of human development through longitudinal studies, cross-sectional studies, cross-cultural studies, experimental studies, although all these kinds of studies—*carried out with the telos of "development"*

---

[6]The plagiarism comes from various of my papers in Wapner and Kaplan (1983) and in Lerner (Kaplan, 1983c).

in mind—may help us to recognize our own egocentricities, ethnocentricities, *préjuges du monde*; and may provide us with information about factors, at any and all levels of analysis, that facilitate or impede human development. *I empha-size the necessity for having the telos of "development" in mind:* It entails, in my view, that developmentalists specify how their inquiries and the results of their inquiries bear on issues of human freedom, liberation, perfection.

Far be it from me to assume or suggest that the proposed telos of development is transparent or easy to articulate. The nature of human perfection and human freedom have been problematic throughout history. Mortimer Adler (1958, 1961) has devoted two thick volumes to summarizing the diverse and conflicting views of philosophers on the nature and conditions for human freedom and has surely omitted many important contributions to the debate. This suggests that one of the tasks of those concerned with human development is to work to clarify the teloi and ultimate telos of human development. And such a work inevitably involves those of us who are psychologists with the writings of all of those who have concerned themselves with that issue: anthropologists, sociologists, econo-mists, philosophers, historians, and so on. Human development is too important to be left to the psychologists and also too important to be parcelled out and fragmented among disciplines segregated from each other.

Permit me now to return to some of the troublesome issues that I left dangling before, troublesome issues that I may have created for myself.[7] Here I am advancing a universal telos for human development—whether freedom, perfec-tion or what not—and all along, I have been suggesting that teloi and the ordering of values for characterizing ideal human development are, in fact, variable over sociocultural groups, and even variable over individuals compris-ing sociocultural groups. We may all agree that human development is a nor-mative concept, a value concept. And yet some (many? most?) will insist, as a matter of principle, an ethical or axiological matter, that one ought not to impose transcendent teloi and values (which it is said *must* mask the teloi and values of one's own culture or one's self) on other sociocultural groups or other indi-viduals. To do so would be ethnocentric or egocentric, and presumably, as a matter of values, one *ought not* to be so. It is implied, in this critique, that cultures and ultimately individuals are absolute monarchs. One might say, for instance, as a matter of dispassionate observation, that Occidentals and Orientals have different conceptions of the character of ideal moral development or ideal person development. Or again, perhaps counterfactually, that men and women have different conceptions of the character of ideal moral development or ideal person development. Or, more generally, different groups may have different standards or norms for what constitutes the traditional triune deity—the True, the Good, and the Beautiful—all values it should be noted. If such values are

---

[7]See, for what follows, my paper "Reflections on culture and personality from the perspective of Genetic-Dramatism" in Wapner and Kaplan (1983).

culture-bound or relative to individuals, who are we—where is our authority—to suggest transcendent values that ought to operate in the lives of all human beings? One may extend this argument, of course, to the jurisdiction of "societies" or "representatives of societies" over individuals in a social group. Where is the authority of parents, teachers, and so on to impose their values on others? Ultimately, is all talk of human development merely a cover for the exercise of power?

Now, there is no contesting that arguments against transcendent teloi and values seem to have an intrinsic appeal to many of us, as long as we adopt the role of spectators (as opposed to actors) with regard to sociocultural scenes (Beck, 1975). We have come to believe that the values of "good," "right," and "beautiful" are subjective or relative. And although some of us hold on to transcendent norms and values of the "rational" and the "true," there seems to be no good reason to exempt these from the dung heap of the immanent if one tosses the others on to it. Thus, one may argue that no one from an alien culture can legitimately assess as higher or lower, more advanced or less advanced, any practices, beliefs or modes of being in the world of members of another society or social group. All those cross-cultural studies, so beloved by some Western developmental psychologists, applying concepts, methods and elaborate scales to determine the "stages" or "levels" that the aborigines attain, are merely ethnocentric impositions that seek to squeeze others into the Procrustean bed of one's own parochial value categories. In sum, one really has no justification for speaking of the level of cognitive development, moral development, development of concepts of justice, self, or anything else with respect to practices and beliefs of a sovereign sociocultural order other than the one to which one belongs.

If, following this purgative thesis to its sour-tasting end, we decide to abjure the imposition of all value judgments on denizens of another social order (and ultimately other individuals), the only unbiased way open to us seems to be provided by *met hodos* of positivistic science. Let us eliminate values from our inquiry and stick only to the objective facts of change over the life span. We may of course take, among the facts of change, the adoption by individuals of certain values of their social order at certain periods in the life span, but these would not be norms *for us* but only normative facts *about them*—facts about their attitudes and beliefs at different periods, and facts about the real factors that determine such value attitudes and beliefs. With respect to the "development" of human beings in societies, this posture would seem to entail characterizing the changes that occur in some *naturally* given entity, or some "natural" aspect or part of that entity in the course of time. The "natural entity," naturally taken as the object of description, is the human being: sometimes from birth to senescence; sometimes from conception to the omega point. The selected aspects of the human being—e.g., breathing, remembering, fantasizing, reasoning—are arbitrary only in their selection. They are otherwise given as natural aspects of the natural entity.[8]

The job of the developmental psychologist, on the Way, is to describe, without prejudice, the ways in which given human beings (as natural wholes) or their aspects or parts (as natural parts) change "as a function of" changes taking place either in the parts, or in the naturally given environments that surround the human being. Through various "operations" on their observations of these patterns of change, the developmentalist, as describer of the facts, is able to offer a factual, value-free representation of the nature of human development.[9]

Now, some descriptive developmentalists (D-Ds), in our society or civilization, observing that changes in human form and behavior correlate variably with selected aspects of human beings and varying features of the "environment," have sought to go beyond the descriptions of individual human beings changing as a function of *x, y* and *z*. Through a range of conceptual, methodological, and statistical operations,[10] presumed to be innocent of any charges of child molesting, these D-Ds have presented us with a description of *the development of the child* or, more recently, *the development of the human being over the life span.* Through these descriptions, we have ostensibly learned about *the* moral development of the child, *the* language development of the child, *the*—fill it in— development of the child; soon to be heard from, doubtless, are those who will give us pure factual descriptions of *the*—fill it in—development of the individual over the life span, demonstrating the relationships of all "variables" to all other "variables."

It is partly against the *definite article* that many D-D anthropologists and an increasingly large number of de-centered psychologists have launched their at-

---

[8]On the changing nature of "the natural," see Lovejoy (1948/1952); Lovejoy and Boas (1935/1965); also Abrams (1955, 1971); Collingwood (1945). The assumption of natural, unmediated, givens (as wholes or parts) to be the objects of factual description already entails the imposition of a perspective in apparently neutral descriptive enterprise. See Whitehead (1938); Polanyi (1962). Those who assert that some object is naturally given characteristically take their terministic screen as "literal" (Cirillo & Kaplan, 1983).

[9]Some will maintain that we are here characterizing and belaboring a "straw man." No investigator—developmental psychologist or anthropologist—believes today that this is what he or she is doing. This may be the case with respect to proclaimed beliefs, but we question whether it is so with regard to the tacit presuppositions. Surely, there are some today, raising the straw man charge, who consider the "human being" as a "natural object" and the actions, aspects of action and characteristics of the environments observed and correlated by the investigator as given to the "innocent eye" (as data). Indeed, they may even deny that the objects of their investigations are the objects of their construction, while concurrently maintaining the "constructivist nature of all human cognitive activity."

[10]One might suggest that theoretical or descriptive concepts are "instruments" and "terministic screens" (Burke) and, so too, are methods. These are likely to disturb and perturb the "facts," giving rise to new "facts" or "facts" that would never come to light without their interventions. This fact, although sometimes acknowledged, is, in fact, often repressed by adulators of the "facts."

tack. One cannot talk about *the* development—in a factual, descriptive sense—of anything unless one has examined, comparatively and cross-culturally, human beings who are members of other cultures than one's own. Through such examination, executed *without the importation of ethnocentric* categories,[11] one might find—indeed, one is likely to find—different patterns of human development, in general, and child development, in particular.[12] As long as one follows Spinoza, and shuns ridicule or condemnation, seeking only to understand, one has the opportunity, through cross-cultural study, to determine whether there is one *the* development of the child, or several *the* developments of the child; likely, the latter, since there is considerable evidence of several different such developments of the child in one's native society. Propelled far enough by this "latitudinarianism" one might even discover, with omniscient observers doing the descriptions, that there are almost as many developments as there are human beings. Some D-Ds might even conclude that individual longitudinal studies—impartial biographies of everyone—is the only way to go if one really wants to respect cultural and, finally, individual differences in human development.[13]

One might think such a proposal is a figment of a fevered imagination and a jaundiced eye: an attempt at satire, caricature, and ridicule.[14] But are there not D-Ds today, especially among the burgeoning life-span movement,[15] who suggest that "human development" can only be dealt with adequately if one employs a multiperspectival, multivariate approach? Who believe that the only way to come to valid conclusions about the nature of human development is by examining the functional relationships of everything to everything else from a multiplicity of (professionally respectable) perspectives? (See Kaplan, 1983b) Ostensibly, through such a procedure, we will be enabled to construct a Tower up to the sky, and thereby reach the Empyrean, where the Omniperspectival dwells; or compile an infinitely expandable collection of facts that the Om-

---

[11]To anticipate briefly what is to come later, the very conceptual categories of an observer, taken as if they were universal rather than parochial, constitute an "ethnocentric" if not "egocentric" importation. Strangely enough, this seems to be recognized more clearly when academics apply their conceptual categories to members of sub-cultures within their own society. All description is theory—and hence, perspective—laden (see Goethe, "All fact is already theory.").

[12]One might even find that the definition of the human being, taken as a "natural object" to be studied, turns out to be culturally-symbolically constituted. The anthropologist or cross-cultural psychologist who presupposes the naturalness of the human being and the human life span as the objects of investigation may, in the process of trying to overcome ethnocentrism, be ethnocentric in spite of himself/herself.

[13]Recall William Blake's admonition: "To generalize is to be an idiot; individuality is the alone distinction of merit."

[14]As Art Buchwald has observed and demonstrated time and again, the possibilities of satire are sharply limited by the actualities of life.

[15]It should be emphasized that a "movement" is not a theory or even a perspective. It is doubtless salutary to observe that human life may not terminate with, or remain static after, infancy, childhood, or even adolescence. But that insight surely does not constitute a perspective, although it may derive from a point of view.

niperspectival can encompass in a unified theory. Without pretending ourselves, as human beings, to come to any conclusions about the nature of human development, we can at least provide all the pieces from our different jig-saw puzzles so that an eventual Master Builder may fit them all together in one magnificent structure. By enjoining that each investigator stick to the facts, we can ensure that the final picture will be uncontaminated by values, having no place in the world of facts.

The major problem with this attempt to achieve a non-normative, nonethnocentric characterization of human development is, it seems to me, the failure on the part of those pursuing the facts to realize that facts are not data. As already noted, facts are not given but made, and their making involves categories and methods that are of parochial provenance, and thereby inherently ethnocentric. Ingredient in the very language of the outsiders who do the investigating, no matter how much they seek to be insiders, are value distinctions (cf. Louch, 1960), alien to the scenes in which the insiders live. This is even more the case when the outsiders (cross-cultural psychologists, anthropologists) go beyond "description" to "explanation," invoking "metaphors" and "terministic screens" derived from their own scenes of participant-action, their own schemas of making sense, which they take to have some universal warrant and transcendent value (See Pepper, 1942).

Much as I would like to pursue these issues further (Wapner & Kaplan, 1983), time runneth out; I can only hope that they will be discussed after my paper today or in the general conference this afternoon.

Before I close, I must address the issue of the telos or value I have proposed. I have already indicated how difficult it is to arrive at a clear meaning of such terms as freedom, emancipation, liberation, perfection. Obviously one must confront considerations of freedom from and for what, perfection of what, and so on. Among the assassins—at least in caricature—it may have been the supreme value to move toward perfection in killing someone. And one may approximate perfection in any social role or occupation—pickpocketry, pornography, or polo—without such near-perfection contributing to one's perfection as a human being. Indeed, sometimes perfection with regard to a lower order telos or value may militate against development as a human being.

I have been especially chided by someone I take to be a major descriptive-developmentalist for suggesting, at one point, "freedom" as the telos of human development. Inaccurately attributing to me the notion of freedom in the sense of the liberation of the individual from all constraints—being able to do one's thing in terms of one's sovereign values irrespective of others—he suggested that other social groups take community values as their highest teloi—taking it as a value to subordinate one's own striving to a larger whole. In some Western traditions, e.g., among neo-Hegelians like Bradley, Bosanquet, and others, this kind of subordination of the individual to a larger whole has been taken as a "higher freedom," indeed, the true route to freedom.

I stop here. Clearly with regard to a telos of a clear, well-organized paper, this is a relatively primitive one. It needs considerable work to become more perfect, to be more fully developed. Alas, and happily, one can console oneself with the realizing the truth of that profound classic cliché—NO ONE IS PERFECT.

REFERENCES

Abrams, M. H. (1955). *The mirror and the lamp*. New York: Oxford.

Abrams, M. H. (1971). *Natural supernaturalism*. New York: W. W. Norton.

Adler, M. J. (1958). *The idea of freedom* (Vol. 1). New York: Doubleday.

Adler, M. J. (1961). *The idea of freedom* (Vol. 2). New York: Doubleday.

Beck, L. W. (1975). *The actor and the spectator*. New Haven: Yale University Press.

Berlin, I. (1954). *Historical inevitability*. London: Oxford University Press.

Black, M. (1954). The definition of scientific method. In M. Black (Ed.), *Problems of anlaysis*. Ithaca: Cornell University Press.

Burke, K. (1945). *A grammar of motives*. Englewood Cliffs, NJ: Prentice-Hall.

Cassirer, E. (1961). *Logic of the humanities*. New Haven: Yale University Press.

Cirillo, L., & Kaplan, B. (1983). Figurative action from the perspective of Genetic-Dramatism. In S. Wapner & B. Kaplan (Eds.), *Toward a holistic developmental psychology*. Hillsdale, NJ: Lawrence Erlbaum Associates.

Collingwood, R. G. (1945). *The idea of nature*. New York: Oxford University Press.

Kaplan, B. (1983a). Reflections on culture and personality from the perspective of Genetic-Dramatism. In S. Wapner & B. Kaplan (Eds.), *Toward a holistic developmental psychology*. Hillsdale, NJ: Lawrence Erlbaum Associates.

Kaplan, B. (1983b). Genetic-Dramatism: Old wine in new bottles. In S. Wapner & B. Kaplan (Eds.), *Toward a holistic developmental psychology*. Hillsdale, NJ: Lawrence Erlbaum Associates.

Kaplan, B. (1983c). Some problems and issues for a theoretically-oriented life-span developmental psychology. In R. Lerner (Ed.), *Developmental psychology: Historical and philosophical perspectives*. Hillsdale, NJ: Lawrence Erlbaum Associates.

Kaplan, B. (1983d). *Strife of systems. Rationality and irrationality in development*. Worcester, MA: Clark University Press.

Louch, A. R. (1960). *Explanation and human action*. Berkeley: University of California Press.

Lovejoy, A. O. (1948/1952). *Essays in the history of ideas*. Baltimore: Johns Hopkins Press.

Lovejoy, A. O., & Boas, G. (1935/1965). *Primitivism and related ideas in antiquity*. New York: Octagon Books.

Löwith, K. (1949). *Meaning in history*. Chicago: University of Chicago Press.

Mills, C. W. (1959). *The sociological imagination*. New York: Oxford University Press.

Northrop, F. S. C. (1947). *The logic of the sciences and the humanities*. New York: Macmillan.

Pepper, S. (1942). *World hypotheses*. Berkeley: University of California Press.

Polanyi, M. (1962). *Personal knowledge*. New York: Harper.

Popper, K. (1957). *The poverty of historicism*. London: Routledge & Kegan Paul.

Russell, E. S. (1982). *Form and function*. Chicago: University of Chicago Press. (Originally published 1916)

Stevenson, C. L. (1944). *Ethics and language*. New Haven: Yale University Press.

Wapner, S., & Kaplan, B. (Eds.). (1983). *Toward a holistic developmental psychology*. Hillsdale, NJ: Lawrence Erlbaum Associates.

Watkins, M. (1982). *The development of imaginal dialogues*. Unpublished doctoral dissertation, Clark University, Worcester, MA.

Weber, M. (1977). Objectivity in social science and social policy. In F. Dallmayr & T. McCarthy (Eds.), *Understanding and social inquiry.* Notre Dame, IN: Notre Dame University Press.

Werner, H. (1937). Process and achievement: A basic problem of education and developmental psychology. *Harvard Educational Review, 7,* 353–368.

Whitehead, A. N. (1938). *Modes of thought.* New York: Macmillan.

Wild, J. (1966). The concept of human existence. *Monist, 50,* 1–16.

DISCUSSION

BRUNER: Some of you will remember a book by Isaiah Berlin, which was called *The Hedgehog and the Fox*. It had as its motto a piece from the Greek poet Archilocus which said, in effect, the fox knows many things, the hedgehog knows one big thing. He then went into an analysis of the philosophy of history in which he compares Tolstoy and Carlisle and their approaches to history. I had a great insight in listening to Bernie. There is only one kind of fox; they believe that knowledge is driven by observation and data, that you go and find lots of things, and that's the lots of things that the fox knows. However, I think I have detected that there are two kinds of hedgehogs. One kind I want to call the substantive or product hedgehog, and the other I want to call the process hedgehog. The product hedgehog says, for example, like Thomas Hobbes, that the nature of human nature is the war of all against all— he's taking some substantive things; or the basis of humankind is a natural goodness, a kind of Franciscan version of the thing; or the telos that one inevitably moves toward. Curiously, in the midst of Jerry Kagan's foxery I also noticed some product hedgehogery about the way in which human beings would develop to avoid anxiety, boredom, uncertainty, and so forth.

Let me say a word about the two kinds of hedgehogs. Part of the feeling of disenchantment [is] with developmental psychologies that assume that there is one way up, one kind of human nature that will express itself but for the fact that there are interfering injustices, degradations, or differential opportunities that prevent its coming up. There is another view. If you place your emphasis upon the process whereby people coming into any culture have somehow to renew it, have to negotiate values, have to restipulate what they shall take as reality, no matter what the content, there is an inevitable set of processes, and those processes create the opportunities for growth or the tragedies of growth. I think we've wasted an enormous amount of effort battling the ideological issue as to what is the essential product, the nature of human nature. I don't think that as psychologists we have spent enough time talking about the processes whereby people achieve such maturity as they are going to be able to achieve, such final state, telos, or whatnot. It's for that reason that I think we have got to break away from the kind of thing that leads us to that dispositional analysis of what the nature of human nature is. I think we're stuck with the idea that somehow the basic problem of human nature is to talk about what's inside a skin—that the skin somehow defines what the task of the psychologist is. Much of what we do is trans-individual. We enter upon a stage in which a play is already going on, and most plays have some universality. So, I hope that we won't get stuck in talking about original human nature but the processes by which human beings achieve this final state, which I'm not altogether prepared to call telos, but whatever you call it.

KAPLAN: Could I make just one remark on what you had to say. I remember the Archilocus fragment, and it was that "the hedgehog knows one thing but knows it well."

BRUNER: No, no, that's your gloss. [Laughter]

BERNSTEIN: What keeps coming to mind is an old union song, "Which side are you on?" It becomes clear what you're against and why you are against it. In a certain interpretation, I myself am very sympathetic. But what you are for seems to me much more ambiguous. Let me reiterate your own definition of developmental psychology and then point out what you pointed out are some of the problems with it. You said that developmental psychology is a practical, theoretical discipline, a policy discipline, concerned with the perfection, including the liberation or freedom, of the individual and the perfection of those modes of operation promoting the perfection of the individual. Now, let's accept this. It seems to me what you are constantly pointing out in the paper is the way many of the key terms you are using—*perfection, freedom, liberation*—are counters or open variables. Indeed, you could be read as deconstructing what you were saying because you were saying as soon as we become determinate about what we really mean by liberation, or freedom, or perfection, we are involved in a whole host of disputes. What you didn't do is give any clue to how one would give a developmental approach to which conceptions of perfection, liberation, or freedom are to be preferred or are higher. In that sense, your paper can be read as if it were stating a hedgehog position but you are constantly undermining it or raising deep skeptical questions. If one wanted to be a kind of malicious relativist one could say that's really relativism manqué.

KAPLAN: I think in some respects that's a just statement. That's what I was in part doing when I wrote this paper. What I'm struggling with is obviously what you referred to yesterday as the issue of historicity and at the same time whether we have to assume with regard to human beings that there is a capacity for transcendence of historical limits in some way. Even the claim to historicity that you raised yesterday already involves a truth claim that supposedly transcends history. In that way, it's not to say "I at this point in time say this or so and so," but "This is true throughout." I think that this is a problem for most of the relativists. I don't want to be presumptuous and dogmatic with respect to determining the telos. I might take Carol's suggestion, taking it as an ideal the community of equals will determine, with regard to a whole host of other things, what constitutes perfection. I take perfection in that way, to be something that we cannot know but operates as a regulative principle or an ideal that we try to articulate. In some domains it is very easy to articulate. With regard to occupations, for example, whether we think that the ultimate teloi are valuable or not, we have standards of perfection that we take for granted and that most people who play the game would take for granted. What does it mean to be a scientist? for example. And what does it mean with regard to steps toward being a scientist by examining individuals who claim to be so doing? We posit a standard and we assess the progress toward it. This is a much more difficult thing, we're suggesting, with regard to the more ultimate teloi. I cannot give you a specification. You're right. It's not that it's relative. We have to struggle to try to come to some conclusion, but we do not because people believe the alternatives say, "Well, each is as good as the other." That doesn't completely address your question, but maybe you want to pursue it.

BERNSTEIN: I think there is more substance underlying it that has not been made explicit. The notion of perfection without qualification is so empty that I think you really have a determinate idea of perfection which is not made explicit. Of course, you don't want to speak about a perfect bureaucrat; you don't want to speak about the perfect expert; you don't want to speak about the perfect manager. You want to in some ways order these conceptions and say there are certain conceptions of perfection which are wrong, bad, inadequate. That's what I think has to be said.

KAPLAN: Yes. As some of you know, in other papers I have suggested that the ideal perfection, if you like Feuerbach's "God is Man's alienated essence," is to be God. that's difficult enough—to give God determinate characteristics.

BRUNER: That begs the same question.

KAPLAN: That's right. Yes.

GILLIGAN: Yesterday first Dick and then I raised the question of are we caught between only two alternatives? Either there is one god or there are an endless number of gods. It seems to me that's the problem. Either there is a single telos or there is no way to choose among the endless array.

KAPLAN: Including demons, I take it?

GILLIGAN: Including demons and so forth. Let me try my own position on you in this context. There are two value potentials that are embedded in the structure of human relationships: one toward whatever you call freedom, emancipation, liberation, individual perfection; the other, toward care and community. This is inherent in the very structure of human relationship. Then, why do we want to reduce it? You get a line that says freedom, emancipation, liberation, perfection; you anticipate the criticism from the other dimension; you say by freedom I mean freedom to care. It's the pull that you can't solve the problem unless you can have a single end. It seems to me that the theoretical, the structural point is: why the either/or of either one or an endless array?

KAPLAN: Let me put it this way. Let's assume we could take, since we are determining what's inherent in human nature, a whole range of others. Why not have not only two but a multiplicity of deities?

GILLIGAN: Let me add one more thing. I guess my own question that's being focused by this conference is, Can developmental psychology tell us something about value presuppositions as well as be criticized by a philosophy of science that is very sensitive to these issues?

KAPLAN: It may be able to tell us something about value presuppositions. It's a question of whether it tells us something about ultimate values and whether we read those off from what we take to be human nature or not.

GILLIGAN: But there I think *you* have the answer because from what standpoint does one read off ultimacy? There is none.

KAPLAN: Therefore we can say it's a dogma. I happen to agree with you, as you know. Then, the standard of perfection has to include not these two as separate but their relationship to each other. In other words, it's a more complex notion in that way, the liberation of the individual and the respect for the community but they . . .

GILLIGAN: But then you are going to translate both of them into the form of one. The liberation of the individual or the perfection of the individual and the attachment of that individual . . .

KAPLAN: No, the perfection of the individual includes both.

GILLIGAN: But then you have to have an image of relationship.

KAPLAN: Of course. I don't think the image of relationship is agreement. I think that's where we get in trouble. The image of relationship could be dialogue, tension, drama, so that it doesn't reduce because it's only if your image of relationship is agreement that in the end the two come to one. Let me take it then one step further. What if the image is disagreement? Then, in that sense, let's say there is constant tension.

GILLIGAN: Yes, why not use the word *conversation?*

KAPLAN: But, let's say one does not want to converse.

GILLIGAN: I think that's a key question.

KAPLAN: At that point you are saying for you the conversation of equals is the highest value. All right? That's the one.

BRUNER: If you keep a focus on the notion of relationship and the requiredness of the relationship's working out in some fashion, you have to take these two things into account. Both your notion of achieving a perfection and achieving this care relationship.

KAPLAN: I think I'm in agreement with you, and I thought that's what I was suggesting when I said taking both of those into account, they then become the specification of perfection.

BRUNER: But then it has to be said I would agree with Richard. You [speak] in such general forms that it doesn't take into account these two pressing structural requirements.

KAPLAN: What you're helping me to do, and Richard is helping me to do, is exactly to try to specify further what is essential. We're not going to find that by simply investigating what takes place in different groups. Therefore, it involves more than psychologists, more than any group, to try operating in the mode that you [Gilligan] take to be so central. This is what we take; we may be in history but we take it to be transcendent. We may find in the course of history that we have to qualify what we have taken to be transcendent. We are constantly engaged in that. That's what I mean when I say it's an ideal to which we point and I think it's necessary to put that against the opposition that there are multiple teloi.

KAGAN: Our species is given a competence we call knowing. I assume the primary purpose of the use of mind is to serve that function. I am perfectly willing to agree, if you find it helpful, with a transcendent telos. I don't choose to do so because it doesn't help me. But what I don't understand is why you are so certain that a descriptive developmentalist who does not choose that form has to be incorrect. That's what I don't understand.

KAPLAN: I do not mean to suggest that they are incorrect because incorrect already implies certain standards of what constitutes the domain. A lot of descriptive developmentalists may be studying the history of the individual. I am proposing, prescriptively, a different constitution of the concept of development that is probably more in accord with what we mean by that in everyday life before we become professional psychologists. That doesn't mean you're incorrect. From my point of view that is not doing developmental psychology although it may be doing very profound history.

Let me say another thing with regard to your question. Part of what we have is cultural variation in what constitutes knowing. We take as transcendent what distinguishes knowing from anything else. Even though in a particular society say that's how we get insight into the structure of the self and the structure of nature, you say, no, that's not knowing.

KAGAN: I don't say that.

KAPLAN: You don't? So you take your form of knowing as only one possible . . .

KAGAN: That's why I made one of the suppositions what you call personal-impersonal, what I called subjective-objective. There are two frames of knowing.

KAPLAN: We can say, fine, we're adopting what we take to be an impersonal mode. Then you might argue that any other society, that their impersonal will not be what we call the scientific mode. In other words, we stipulate what constitutes science. It's not a discovery out in the world. Someone stipulates what we take to be a legitimate scientific mode of knowing and we stipulate what the categories are of that.

KAGAN: Why do you keep inserting the word *scientific?* It is all irrelevant. You want to define categories the way a scholastic does. It's of no help whatsoever. For a man who prizes freedom as a goal, for you to categorically say you cannot do that . . .

KAPLAN: I didn't say you cannot do that. I say what you do, do.

KAGAN: But I don't understand. If you're such a proponent of freedom why do you adopt such a posture? What some people should not do . . .

KAPLAN: I did not say you should not do it. I may raise a question about its developmental status, but I did not say you should not do it.

KAGAN: But of what help is it, Bernie, for you or anyone to decide what developmental psychology is? That's totally irrelevant. It's of no help to decide what developmental psychology is.

KAPLAN: I think it is important to have some kind of specification of what the field of discourse is so that at least people are in that sense dealing with the same domain of discourse.

KAGAN: Bernie, let me give an example. Someone found that in a species of coral fish living off the Great Barrier Reef, where a male has a harem of half a dozen females who are in a hierarchy, if the male dies the female who is dominant undergoes a morphological transformation and becomes male. Does that phenomenon belong under psychology or biology? The answer is, "Who the hell cares?" It's irrelevant to what domain it belongs.

KAPLAN: But see, then we can raise a question . . .

BERNSTEIN: I think there's a way of stating your point so maybe there's not so much difference. Maybe this is too generous to you, Bernie.

KAPLAN: That's okay. I can take generosity. [Laughter]

BERNSTEIN: I think what you are distressed with is a real tendency. I think the issue is not scholastic—you are trying to define what kind of field and saying ''you are outside that field, you might be doing something else''—but rather a serious problem and a deep confusion that does occur in developmental work. One doesn't have to negate that there is some value in longitudinal studies, that there is a point to cross-cultural kinds of analyses, but it is true that if you look at the history of developmental psychology there has been sometimes very blatantly that enormous tendency towards reification, that enormous tendency to make the slippage from something that may be of local or parochial significance, of historical significance, as if we are discovering something more. That's the danger, that you can somehow make that kind of move in which you really think that the facts will tell us what is development. That's not a pseudo-issue because I think one can document how much, in sophisticated or in blatant forms, this has been a tendency in the history of developmental psychology. Is that fair?

KAPLAN: Yes. I wanted to add something to this. I am not saying here is a fixed domain, because there are artificial divisions between disciplines. I'd say it's as important for developmental psychology, taking up what Jerry [Bruner] said before, not to treat development as a subcutaneous phenomenon in the same sense, as Dewey, Cassirer and others said, that mind is at least as much a matter of culture as it is of the individual, which means that we may have to include within developmental psychology—and then we might call it developmental anthropology or something else—a whole range of institutions that are treated as if they have nothing to do with human mental functioning because they have to do with law, religion, all the things that people used to call the objective mind. I am saying that we are still concerned in that sense insofar as we talk about development. Now you may disagree and say ''I talk about development as the equivalent for history.'' I am trying to separate off talk about some movement toward teloi.

AUDIENCE MEMBER: I was intrigued by your notion of teloi, making them independent of time. Say more about that.

KAPLAN: I try to distinguish development from ontogenesis and history, what actually happens. An ideal form doesn't mean it has a sort of subsistence independent of human beings doing something, but operates as an assessment of what takes place in ontogenesis. That kind of distinction is necessary it seems to me to use terms such as *regression, arrest,* and so on. In that sense, I am saying that you can't read it off from what takes place in the course of time.

BRUNER: Is telos in your head, in the organism, where?

KAPLAN: The whole tone of contemporary treatment of values is that values are subjective. Obviously that's opposed to a tradition which tried to find out an objectivity of value. Partly with the death of God, I guess, we got this assumption that values are simply subjective. That easily becomes values— true, good, beautiful—are all a matter of taste. Usually that statement is made as a true statement that is not a matter of taste. When we say, ''Values are a matter of taste,'' we say what I say now is not a matter of taste but happens to be the truth and the absolute, transcendent truth. So part of the struggle will be: Can we establish certain kinds of values and on what basis? I don't claim we can, you understand, because I'm as much a product of these historical circumstances as anybody else. I don't take it that I'm determined in that way. I am trying to transcend that.

KAGAN: What's your answer to Jerry's question. Where are they?

KAPLAN: I would say when we posit such values, they are mandatory. I don't want to start with the subject; they are demands made on us.

KAGAN: They're external to you?

KAPLAN: They're external to me.

AUDIENCE MEMBER: Yours are in the Constitution of the United States.

KAPLAN: Mine are in the Constitution?

AUDIENCE MEMBER: Your teloi.

BRUNER: Freedom. The right to . . .

KAPLAN: Now, do you think they're beyond that? That's the question.

KAGAN: You do.

KAPLAN: I do.

KAGAN: You're brave to answer.

KAPLAN: Even those have to be specified, but there are certain values that I take to be mandatory.

6

On the Creation and Transformation of Norms of Human Development

Marx W. Wartofsky
Baruch College

INTRODUCTION

In the second edition of Mussen, Conger, and Kagan's *Readings in Child Development and Personality*—i.e., in 1970—the editors write in the preface:

> Many of the papers reflect a major conceptual change that has occurred in recent years. We now view the mind of the child as active and constructive, rather than as an empty blackboard, a *tabula rasa* upon which the message of experience is written. We see the infant and young child as a highly structured organism, trying to make sense of his experience, not as a piece of clay passively molded by social forces. (p. XII)

In Wilhelm Preyer's *Die Seele des Kindes,* published in 1881 (Preyer 1881/1965), we read:

> The mind of the new-born child, . . . does not resemble a *tabula rasa,* upon which the senses first write their impressions . . . but the tablet is already written on before birth . . . [By careful observation of the child] we perceive what a capital each individual has inherited from his ancestors—how much there is that is not produced by sense-impressions, and how false is the supposition that man learns to feel, to will, and to think only through his senses. (p. 132)

One may infer that the "major conceptual change" that had "occurred in recent years" in 1970 had also occurred at least once before, almost a century earlier. And indeed, this major conceptual change had already occurred several times over, in the centuries before that. "Plus ça change, plus ça change" might be the moral of this tale. But my intention here is not to pose as a historical know-it-all and smirk at historically naive claims to theoretical innovation. Nor is it to enter the maze of the nature-nurture or cognitivist-behaviorist or a priori-empiricist controversies once again. Rather, I want to stand aside and muse on the following proposition: that psychological theories of learning, of growth, of development themselves contribute to *shape* the modes of learning, growth, development which they are about and that, therefore, the psychological theorist bears the burden of *constituting,* in part at least, how child development, or human development, as an actual phenomenon or process will take place. To put this more explicitly or perversely, I want to explore and defend the claim that human beings themselves create and transform the norms of development and that such norms effectively influence (though they do not fully determine) how infants, children, and the rest of us will, in fact, develop. The general thesis here is that we are a self-constituting species and that our self-constitution proceeds by the choices we make among alternative, possible modes of praxis, whether we distinguish these as modes of action, perception, or thought; whether we assign such practices to the domains of social interaction, morals, art, science, education, medicine, play, or sport. Among the most significant of such choices among modes of praxis we may make is that of theory: for as a theoretical species—as *homo sapiens* or *homo theorens*—we have evolved cognitively to the point where our self-conscious self-characterizations—what we take ourselves to be, how we conceive of our capacities, our ends, our goods—function as feedback into the very modes of further practice that we develop; and that these ways of doing, acting, making, perceiving, understanding effectively constitute us as the kinds of beings we are, and shape or transform our natures.

Theory-laden observation in science is therefore only one mode of the theory-laden-life-activity that distinguishes our cognitive species from others. Thus, the bald thesis that I want to examine here is that theories of development, and thus, alternative or even antithetical theories of development, contribute to the shaping of alternative or even antithetical modes of actual development. Self-conscious, cognitive, theoretically oriented practice enters as a dynamic variable into the mechanisms of cultural evolution, in a way that adds to, and also supersedes, the mechanisms of interaction that characterize biological evolution. We are, in effect, a self-creating species; which is to say, we mark the alternative possible paths of our development with the norms we ourselves propose and adopt as proper to that development.

Now this is a highly constructivist thesis, stated here in its strongest form, and it raises some sharp and obvious problems.

For example: Are the *facts* of human development (e.g. the "hard facts" of physiological maturation or the "soft facts" of cognitive growth) simply at the mercy of any theoretical construction whatever, or are there not, instead, objective features of development which it is theory's task to discover, report, and understand? If the actual phenomena of development are even in part constituted by theory and its effects in its adoption and application (e.g., in education or in social policy, or in evaluative or diagnostic judgments made in therapy or in rehabilitation), then what remains of the epistemological notion of the *truth* of theories of development? For if a theory *about* the social or psychological phenomena of development can, in effect, reconstruct or constitute the domain of its application or its empirical test in accordance with its norms, doesn't theory become self-fulfilling prophecy rather than scientific truth-claim? Or again: If we are a self-constituting species in our patterns or norms of development, are there not, if not biological, then at least cultural or social or technological constraints that set the limits of a theory's applicability or efficacy? If we *do* in fact create ourselves in the image of our own valuative ideals of development, is this a *creatio ex nihilo,* or is this creation shaped by the inherent, or objective, properties of the raw material, or inherited form of being, that is transformed by this creation? These are hard questions, and therefore I will avoid them now and will later add qualifications to the constructivism that I am proposing here, as I slowly lose my nerve and climb back somewhat from the exposed limb I have put myself on. But in these preliminary remarks, I want to draw my thesis in starkest outline and add the *chiaroscuro* as I proceed.

In order to frame this thesis more fully, I propose to address three questions here. The first concerns the normative character of *any* theory of human development. How do theories of development, *volens nolens,* presuppose value presuppositions, how do such normative presuppositions come to be determined, and how do they come to be changed? Second, how do theories of development affect the practices—social, educational, moral, scientific-technological—that shape or change the processes of development themselves? That is, what are the mechanisms of theoretical self-constitution in human development, and what are the limits and constraints of such self-constitution? Third, how do specific, contemporary theories of human development or contemporary research-programs and research-methodologies in this field reflect the parameters of normativeness and of self-constitution addressed in the first two questions?

Because what I am proposing is a framework of the historical creation and transformation of norms of development, let me begin with a historical sketch, or better, schema in which the relation between the practices that shape development and developmental theories may be examined. In general, this may be seen as part of a larger project, which I have called historical epistemology, in which I propose what is, in effect, a constructivist theory of cultural evolution, to the effect that modes of cognition and perception change historically with changes in modes of social, technological, scientific, and artistic praxis. As will be seen, the agency of the interaction between embodied practices or modes of action and forms of thought or of perception is the creation and use of artifacts and, specifically, of what I will call representational artifacts or, in short, representations. Without entering into the question of internal or mental representations (which I have addressed elsewhere) let me make clear that what I have in mind here, so to speak, are *external* forms of representation, representational artifacts, of the sort we usually speak of as linguistic or pictorial artifacts, but which include any made thing or structure that comes to function symbolically—including here tools, social structures or emblems, rules of action, or exemplary models of action or of ways of doing things. In particular, I will be concerned here with *theoretical* representations: scientific theories, explicitly formulated norms (usually expressed in linguistic form), or models of procedure or action.

In this sense, the history of theories of development serves as a history of the ways in which development has been represented theoretically, or to put it in Hegelian jargon, the ways in which human development has itself become an object of consciousness—i.e., the ways in which we have become self-conscious of the processes of our own development (or indeed, of the development of nature as a whole). In this history we may then read back the self-conceptions that have emerged and changed and that, if I am correct, have affected the very nature of human development itself. We have become, in part, what we have taken ourselves to be. But, as I will argue, we do not take ourselves to be just anything we please. The construction of norms of development is no arbitrary or whimsical process (though elements of arbitrariness, whimsy, and the playful imagination surely enter into the construction of such norms). If we are the historical creatures of our own conventions, the self-creating and self-transforming products of our own constructive activity, then the shaping, adoption, and use of such conventions or constructions is a laborious social and cultural process. It is not *merely* historical; it *is* history. So much for grand opening claims. Now, to proceed . . .

A HISTORICAL SCHEMA OF THEORIES
OF DEVELOPMENT

Theories of human development historically have both served as the models for more general conceptions of development—e.g., of natural or social evolution—and have been derived *from* such more general theories. Thus, from the ubiquitous fact of birth as the beginning of human life have emerged metaphors, myths, and theories about the "birth" or genesis of the cosmos, of society, of life in general. The biological kinship of humans and other animals, or even of plants, is one of the earliest sources of concepts of development, such that what was known by humans about themselves was projected as a model of animal life in general, and conversely, human beings took themselves, very early, to be formed in the image of animal life, even identifying their origins and kinship-relations with totem animals, plants, even natural elements. The conception of the world as one great animal, of Being as essentially life-like, was the insight of early hylozoism, in myth and in Greek philosophy and science. So too, the origin, order, and structure of social and political life were cast in the image of human life and also of its cycles of birth, growth, and degeneration, in the earliest cyclic theories of social change.

What is significant for our purposes here is the early struggle between ideas that such development, or cyclic change, was normative (i.e., that the process was not only teleological, or ordered to some end state, but that this end state was *good* or *just* or a fulfillment of potentialities that *ought* to be realized) and the contrary view that the process was blind and, whether the outcome of mere chance or of necessity, value-free and with no end or ultimate aim. Between the normative tradition (e.g., of Platonic and Aristotelian thought) and the non-normative traditions of Democritean or Lucretian atomism or of Stoic and Epicurean theories of natural necessity, human life was seen either as a fulfillment of natural teleology, on the one hand, or as a stoic accommodation to a value-free natural necessity, or contingency. Here, the good in human action lay in the avoidance of pain or conflict and was grounded not in nature but in the conventions of human construction. *Cosmos* and *Nomos* stood, therefore, in uneasy relation in such antithetical approaches. Development as such was either a cosmic imperative, whose good lay in the very nature of things, or it was a choice, whose good lay in our recognition that things were as they were, and that all we could do was to make the best of it. Condemned to be born, to live and to die, by a blind necessity we could invent ways to get along with the least strife, with what limited security the conventions of peace could assure, and with the negative satisfactions of avoiding pain. On this view, there are no values in nature. We create them.

These are large and ancient frameworks, and they persist in their historical transmutations and permutations (for even in their earliest versions, they are not pure, but intermix in complex theoretical ways). Thus, the notion that the norms of development are those that can be established as the innate, natural, or biological propensities of the organism in its life cycle—the realization, in short, of its genetically determined processes—echoes the older ideas of natural necessity and, as we shall see, of natural kinds, which see life as the expression of *cosmos,* in its fixed and differentiated expressions. By contrast, the notion that such developmental norms are historically contingent choices imposed on a plastic nature by conscious beings, or else alternative accommodations to an unfathomable and radically contingent world beyond our control, echoes older conceptions of human life as essentially a construction of *nomos,* a creation of order out of chaos by action and will.

Against this general background, we may schematize three historically crucial notions of development—what we may call "grand theories," because of their generality and because of the influence they have had as models of development across a wide domain: biological, psychological, social. I will label these, crudely, as *Aristotelian* or *essentialist, Darwinian* or *evolutionary,* and *Marxist* or *cultural-historical.* It should be added here that there also exists what one may call a non-developmental theory of development which puts in question any notions of linear or ordered development or teleology, and sees instead a plurality of non-normative sequences with no immanent or overarching pattern. We may call this, variously, *anarchist* or *nihilist* or *deconstructionist,* or in fact, *Dadaist.* It is not so much a *theory* of development as a challenge to the very idea of such theories.

The *Aristotelian* or *essentialist* theory holds that development of any organism, and therefore of humans also, is the unfolding of natural, fixed, or innate potentialities, in the normal process of growth which is distinctive of any given species. Species therefore are, in the Aristotelian language, *natural kinds* or *natures* or *essences:* their being what they are is, in fact, *defined* by the natural process of development. The value-presupposition of such a theory is that the *good* of any organism of a species is its realization of its nature or essence; and that this proceeds as a result of its life-activity, i.e., the kind of activity that *makes* it the kind of thing it is. Development is therefore teleologically fixed as the realization of innate patterns of growth, or *normal* functioning. It is, by definition then, orthogenetic, and defines the *good* of development as development itself, in accordance with one's *nature.* There, of course, is the rub. How does one determine *what* the nature or essence of a given *kind* or *species* is? Aristotle is shrewdly empirical here: We discover this by observation and by practice, through which we may then achieve a scientific knowledge of what is universally necessary. The test of practice, here, is *right functioning,* each thing after its own kind. For human beings, the test of right functioning is well-being, the feeling of pleasure that accompanies the *natural* transition from potentiality to actuality, or of *growth.* We may, with historical hindsight, say, "It depends on what makes you happy, or on what your pleasure is." But Aristotle, as a practicing biologist and a good Athenian citizen, had few qualms here. The threatening circularity of his argument is relieved by the appeal to good sense or reason—the sort any cultivated Greek citizen would share with others, in the catalogue of virtues or modes of right action in accordance with one's nature that marked the *ethos* of Greek life, or that was, in effect, constructed by Aristotle in a self-conscious philosophical articulation of that *ethos,* in a theory persuasive enough to have been used, interpreted, and reinterpreted over two milennia.

But the core of Aristotle's developmental theory is his presupposition of fixed, or essential, natures, as varied as these are in the animal world; and even more, as varied as these may even be among types of individuals (since, in Aristotle's view, there were slaves by nature; and by nature, women were not fully formed men and thus of an incomplete nature.)

That the cultural and social values and biases of the Athenian intellectual are expressed in the metaphysics and social theory of Greek thought is no news; and that these may be traced as well in the theory of development is equally clear. It took no more of a Marxist than John Dewey to recognize this fact, even while acknowledging his deep indebtedness to Aristotelian modes of thought. It takes more of an effort, as I shall argue later, to see the same fact in our own contemporary theories of development.

If the Aristotelian theory of development begins from the conception of fixed natural kinds, so the second *grand* theory of development starts from a sharply different assumption: namely, that the *kinds* or *species* themselves are not fixed, but come into being and pass away; or that species have an origin. The Darwinian, or evolutionary, theory of development is, of course, a biological theory. But its origins are much older and lie beyond modern biology in the notions of the adaptive evolution of forms of life or of forms of Being in ancient Greek thought, e.g., in Empedocles; in highly articulated form in Lucretius; and in the pre-Darwinian vogue of Lucretian evolutionism that marked 18th-century philosophy and biology, e.g., in Maupertuis, in Robinet and Diderot, in Lamarck, and in Erasmus Darwin; and in astronomy, by Laplace's nebular hypothesis on the formation of the planetary system. Side by side with the rationalist essentialism that marked the theories of human nature and the human mind in the tradition from Descartes to Kant, there develops also the double strand of Rousseauian voluntarism and self-constitution with respect to human nature, and Diderotian transformism with respect to biological nature. By the early 19th century the notion of dynamic self-variation of animal and plant species (i.e., the notion of organic evolution) is already widely developed in speculative philosophical and scientific thought; and concomitant notions of the evolution of forms of social life, of language, of forms of thought, also emerge, e.g., in the theories of Vico, Herder, and Hegel. Notions of human development then become bi-polar: in terms of the biological emergence of species, and also in terms of the emergence of varying historical forms of cultural, psycho-social or political-economic life. With Darwin, this burgeoning evolutionary theory finds its natural mechanisms in the theory of natural and sexual selection; and with Spencer and others, the theory is universalized to all domains, and the formal structures of developmental or evolutionary change are elaborated in a new, purportedly scientific metaphysics of change.

Here, development is ambivalently viewed as, on the one hand, the description of a natural, self-acting process of differentiation in response to pressures of environment and population, in which natural selection (or in the phrase which Darwin adopted from Spencer, ''the survival of the fittest'') was an evaluative norm in the guise of a descriptive fact; or on the other, as an explicitly normative and normatively hierarchical account of ''higher'' and ''lower'' orders, of the ''aim'' of evolution, and of orthogenesis, or *right* development, with its connotations of better and worse, normal and pathological, eugenic and dysgenic.

Not only are the fixed, essential Aristotelian natural kinds gone, here, but evolution reveals the teleonomic thrust of the formation of new species and the extinction of older ones; or even further, it reveals the mechanisms by which future evolutionary adaptations may be guided, once we understand how to control them. It is interesting that Darwin begins with an account of the deliberate breeding of domestic animals for certain purposes as evidence of the plasticity of animal forms, though he eschews any notion of final cause or purpose in natural evolution. The values presupposed in the classical evolutionary account of species-development or change remain the biological ones of species-survival, or selective advantage in breeding or reproduction.

The easy adoption of biological evolutionary theory in Germany, compared to the struggle over its acceptance in England and America, is in part due to the fertile conceptual soil of German philosophical and scientific thought in which Darwin's ideas were sown. One important aspect of the evolutionary model of development, as it enters into psychological theory, is the ready mold of German dialectic, from Goethe, Fichte, Schelling, Hegel, Schopenhauer, to Liebig, Moleschott, Buchner and Vogt, among the scientists. Here, the notion that consciousness, or mental life, has a history of self-transforming evolution, that it has stages of development, that it realizes itself more and more fully as it becomes more differentiated, or differentiates *itself* by its own activity—this notion of a dialectic of consciousness, or indeed, of a dialectical *history* of consciousness, was easily accommodated to a notion of organic evolution, of a dialectical unfolding of stages or forms of life. For Schelling, Nature and Spirit were simply two names of the same process, naturalized on the way down, spiritualized on the way up. For Hegel, nature or matter was nothing in itself, but only the other-sidedness, the self-objectification of *Geist*. For Schopenhauer, the world was nothing but the objective, or externalized, form of activity itself, or of the blind self-activity which he called the world-will; organs were nothing but objectified functions; teeth and claws were, in his striking phrase, objectified hunger. Since spirit, will, consciousness is, in these dialectical views, self-active and self-transforming, it was no great strain for a German scientific community brought up on Goethe, Schelling, Hegel, Feuerbach, to adopt a view that living nature is itself not fixed in its species, but is a movement of self-transforming development, in which novelty constantly emerges.

Again, this is significant for our purposes in two very specific ways: In English and American thought, the influence of Darwinian and Spencerian evolutionary models played a crucial role in the shaping of theories of child development, supplemented by the positivist evolutionism which had been adapted from the Comteians, and the dialectical notions inherited by way of literary and scientific romanticism in England from Hegel, Feuerbach, and Schopenhauer. And in France, there developed a strange crypto-Hegelian evolutionism in the Comtean tradition, overlaid with theories of the historical development of stages of consciousness exemplified in the history of science and of mathematics. This, together with its Darwinian, biological interpretations, lies at the roots of the tradition of developmental psychology which passes from Janet to Piaget and through the historical-evolutionary philosophy and history of science and mathematics, in Brunschvicg, Lalande, Meyerson and others.

Thus, Darwinian evolution, German dialectics, and French positivism all feed into a complex model—or better, a set of models—of evolution which becomes a main source of developmental psychology. From Wilhelm Preyer, in Germany, to James Mark Baldwin, G. S. Hall, and John Dewey in the United States, to Janet and others in France, theories of child development took on a distinctively evolutionary cast. But beyond this, the notion of studying human development by way of a study of the development of infants and children received a methodological justification which in effect established the foundations of modern developmental psychology. For on one reading, at least, the child was seen as representing the stages of historical human evolution, in terms of mental life, just as the embryo was seen as representing the stages of biological evolution. If ontogeny recapitulated phylogeny, or even served only as a heuristic guide to its study, then observation of child development was a clue to the evolution of human nature. Moreover, if evolution of species linked humans to their animal forebears, then the child could be taken to represent the more animal-like stages of human development, or conversely, animal life could be taken as the prototype of human life, and animal development, and hence animal-like child life, could be taken as the original root of what evolves as adult life.

William Kessen (1965) writes of this early and ubiquitous notion of "developmental recapitulation":

> From the publication of *The Origin of Species* to the end of the 19th century, there was a riot of parallel-drawing between animal and child, between primitive man and child, between early human history and child. The developing human being was seen as a natural museum of human phylogeny and history; by careful observation of infant and child, one could see the descent of man. . . . The child-as-prototype movement reached its peak with the publication in 1901 of *The Child—A Study in the Evolution of Man* by Alexander Francis Chamberlin. (pp. 115–116)

(Kessen goes on to say "Nothing much is left of this radical notion now." I think he is too sanguine on that score . . . or at least was, in 1965, when he wrote this.)

What is crucial in the Darwinian or evolutionary grand theory of development is not only that it abolishes the idea of fixed or essential species, but that it thereby puts the burden of interpreting or explaining human development squarely upon one or the other, or both, of the two mechanisms of evolution: the evolved genetic structure of the species, as the imprint of its previous adaptation, or the current activity of adaptation to an environment as a means of preserving this evolved genetic structure intact through reproduction. Darwinism had no adequate genetic theory, and Darwin himself opted for what now seems a crudely Lamarckian hypothesis—so-called pangenesis. What his theory provided as a framework for development was natural and sexual selection. "Normal" development, or orthogenesis *within* the species, is therefore determined or defined by whatever preserves the species, i.e., whatever renders it fit for survival as a species. But this is a problematic notion, since survival may dictate species variation, even to the point of *re*speciation, or species change, rather than genetic or specific stability. If the hallmark of Darwinian evolution is in the fact of the fluidity or plasticity of species as a means of the preservation not of *species*-life, but of life itself, even at the "sacrifice," so to speak, of ill-adapted species, then development cannot presuppose, even as a biological norm, the stability or preservation of a species-specific genetic structure. In this way, a developmental norm based on preserving genetic invariance, or reproductive advantage, yields to an ecological genetics, where the norm of development concerns not a *given* form of species-life but planetary life, i.e., inter-specific rather than intra-specific stability.

This bears on questions posed for theories of human development by the latest arguments of the sociobiologists. But since even they—or at least Lumsden and Wilson—have conceded that not merely biological but cultural parameters may play a role here (albeit in the service of the limit-setting genes), we may proceed to that grand theory of development that focuses on the contexts of history and culture as the crucial grounds for developmental theory.

The Marxist theory of development has usually been taken to be a theory of the historical evolution of successive economic formations, or structures of the organization of material life, focused on changes in forces and relations of production as basic, and by derivation from these, on changes in the superstructural forms of social, political, ideological life, and so on. Moreover, in one standard reading, the historical materialism of Marx and Engels, as the paradigmatic early framework of their developmental theory, has been understood as a deterministic and linear unfolding of universal and necessary world-historical stages of the forms of social and economic life. On this reading the Marxian dialectics of development turn out to be, as the critics like to say, mechanistic, objectivistic, historicist (in Popper's critical sense of the term), or positivistic. Though it is true that Marx and Engels sometimes talk in ways which would support such a critical (or even approving) reading, there is a cogent case to be made for a radically different interpretation. I won't make the case here, but offer the alternative reading, because I believe it is truer to the corpus of Marx's thought and because it is this alternative that I am proposing as the case in point of a Marxist "grand theory" of development. It is this: Human beings, unlike animals, create the necessary conditions of their species existence—the production of the means of existence and the reproduction of species life—by means of conscious or cognitive activity, or *praxis*. This praxis is therefore teleological— i.e., it is intentional activity aimed at the satisfaction of perceived needs or historically emergent wants. Therefore, human activity is directed by the imagination or the representation in consciousness of its ends. But the conception of these ends is itself shaped by what, at a given level of cultural, technological, or ideological development, people take to be possible, what they consider their interests and needs to be. It is in the praxis of satisfying such needs that new needs and new possibilities of satisfaction arise. Thus, development in this sense is historical and emergent. It has no predestined telos, or as Marx puts it, human labor or activity has "no predetermined yardstick" but is rather self-transcending and therefore, in Marx's terms, free, or creative, activity: it creates its own ends and, in achieving them, transcends them. In this, says Marx, human *Tätigkeit* (activity, creation, labor—the terms are used interchangeably by Marx) is fundamentally different from the activity of animal life, which is bound by the species-limits of instinct. "Man," says Marx (here echoing Rousseau of the *Essay on the Origins of Inequality Among Men*) "creates in freedom." In doing so, of course, human beings fashion their own chains, in the modes of domination and exploitation that characterize class-societies; and therefore, human beings can break these chains. Marx may be seen, then, as attempting to answer Rousseau's own conundrum, "Human beings are born free. Yet they are everywhere in chains," by a theory of self-development, whose causality is immanent, and results from the agency of the historical forms of human praxis itself.

The theory of development here therefore goes beyond the Aristotelian model of each organism or thing realizing its inherent fixed nature or essence through "normal" activity, given the appropriate conditions; and it also goes beyond the Darwinian evolutionary model of development by adaptation to a given enviroment by variational evolution, i.e., by the formation and change in species through natural selection, by the operations of a will-less and non-teleological nature. What is proposed instead is a pattern of teleological, or consciously purposive, activity in accordance with norms created in the situation of this activity itself; and the transformation and transcendence of any given norms through the very creation of new needs, which this activity occasions.

What is implicit in most of Marx's systematic work, and explicit only occasionally, primarily in the early works, is an utterly Hegelian notion of consciousness, especially as this is developed further by Feuerbach: namely, that human beings create the image of their conscious desires, wants, needs in the objective form of external representations of these desires and then act in accordance with these symbolic objectifications as if they were independently existing imperatives imposed on them from without—by God or by the State or by the moral law or by some other form of external authority. But this externalized, or alienated, mode of the self-representation of human ends or desires is—to use that favorite dialectical locution—"nothing but" the othersidedness of human *self*-consciousness, or in Marx's terms, the projection of the telos of human *praxis,* which, once recognized for what it is, can be reappropriated in the mode of self-determination or freedom, rather than that of determination by some external force or authority. (Thus Marx can speak of Capital as objectified labor, which, under a certain historical form of social organization or of property-relations, appears as an independent, external force upon which labor is itself dependent for its activity.)

The crux of this theory of development is its historicity and its sociality and therefore the historically constructed and variable character of the norms of development. The problem, for the theory, is to discover or understand the process by which such norms come to be established—to be socially legitimated so that they become effective guides or imperatives of human action, and how such norms can be historically changed.

All three grand theories of development—essentialist, evolutionary, and cultural-historical—have this much in common: they serve as theorizations of a certain mode of social life: Aristotle's, of the notion of fixed castes or stations or roles, which one has by nature; thus, a legitimation of the assigned or established hierarchy of social life on grounds that it expresses essential or natural differences among kinds; Darwinism, in its *social* interpretations, as a theorization of social life as itself operating according to the natural laws of fang and claw in the jungle of competition, in the struggle for survival in a context of scarce resources (remember that Darwin derives the grounds of his argument in great part from Malthus' *Essay on Population*) thus legitimating not the fixed *natural* hierarchy, but rather the one that has evolved, where the winners rule because they are the winners; and Marxism, as a theorization of the historicity of *different* "winners," or ruling classes, arising out of the processes of the division of labor and the appropriation of hegemonic control over the means necessary for the production and reproduction of species life.

Aristotle, however, did not *create* Greek society by his theory. It already existed, in a variety of forms, with different sorts of hierarchy. Yet, he provided a model which not only ordered these modes of hierarchy in his theoretical representations of them but also served, in various interpretations, as the legal theory, the ideology and the scientific argument for cognate modes of fixed hierarchical social organization through at least the Middle Ages. Nor did Darwin create the competitive industrial society which mirrored itself in his biological theory (and adapted its lessons about nature in the form of Social Darwinism). Yet, his theory of development certainly served as the model for a biologization of the notions not only of social struggle but also of child development. Similarly, Marx did not invent or create the class struggle or the historicity of the modes of social organization, but he certainly articulated and offered a theoretical construction of these phenomena.

That, however, is not to say that it is theory and its normative or legitimating or critical articulation on the one side, and the hard social facts on the other. The social facts, hard as they may be, are themselves facts constituted by the complex sociocultural processes of self-representation, in all the usual forms in which people take themselves to be what they are, or organize or impose norms of action, moral rules, laws, customs, ideologies, or systems of beliefs. Theorists do not *create* popular or class or moral consciousness; rather this is the complex procedure of the variety of institutions of society. But theorists do two things more than this: They can represent these modes of self-understanding or self-regulation in a determinate, articulated way: they can give this self-understanding voice, so to speak, and reconstruct it rationally, or persuasively, thus legitimating it, or raising it to explicit consciousness; *or* they can serve as critics of the popular or institutional modes of self-understanding and social control, and propose what they consider better alternatives.

Theories of development, therefore, are neither neutral observer reports on the "objective facts" of development, nor are they, in themselves, the arbiters of what will count as development proper, i.e., of "normal" or "good" development. These norms are not simply instituted by theoretical fiat. Rather, they are effected by the social, cultural, political processes of child-rearing, parenting, education, the media; by the whole range of artifacts which, in any given period, come to define the range and character of the accepted or approved modes of child activity or of child development—the forms of dress, the codes of social behavior, the toys and games—in short, all those aspects of culture in which the norms are embodied, preserved, transmitted. Theorists of development do not have the power to determine these norms. But they do have the responsibility to engage in criticism of these norms, in society at large and in self-criticism of theories of development, i.e., of their own normative proposals. They are, moreover, responsible to recognize the historicity or situatedness of these norms and to come down on the right side. In this sense, the theory of child development, as a discipline, should be taken as a branch of social ethics or of critical social theory.[1]

REFERENCES

Kessen, W. (1965). *The child*. New York: Wiley.
Mussen, P., Conger, J., & Kagan, J. (Eds.) (1970). *Readings in child development and personality*. New York: Harper & Row.
Preyer, W. (1965). Expression and the feeling of self. In W. Kessen (Ed.), *The child*. New York: Wiley. (Original work published 1881)
Wartofsky, M. (1983). The child's construction of the world and the world's construction of the child. In F. S. Kessel & A. W. Siegel (Eds.), *The child and other cultural inventions*. New York: Praeger.

---

[1]For a fuller discussion of this see *The Child's Construction of the World and the World's Construction of the Child* (Wartofsky, 1983).

DISCUSSION

KAPLAN: Marx, what is it to come down on the good side, the right side?

WARTOFSKY: I can't tell you what the ''good side'' is in general or abstractly. But I can tell you what *I* think it is, in concrete and specific ways. I'm saying something like what Bernie was saying about the regulative function of this kind of consideration. I think it's part of the agenda or curriculum of the science of developmental psychology to consider how human beings *ought* to develop, that is, to take up the normative question explicitly. How? You engage in a critical discussion, a debate, a fight, a collaboration, an articulation of the issues involved in taking on substantive, normative questions. Someplace, Aristotle said that even in order *not* to do philosophy you have to do philosophy. What I am saying is that the policy science and the theoretical science of development is a normative science. As a normative science it can't simply describe the alternative norms that people *do,* in fact, have (although one may undertake a self-description, a history or critique of contemporary developmental theories to articulate what the alternative norms are that such theories assert, or presuppose). And, by analysis, one may then clarify the claims that are being made. That's step one—the analysis. Then comes the jumping into the water.

I think you can't disengage yourself from actual involvement in the social, political, ethical, moral, ideological discussion of what the *right* kind of development ought to be—including the critical question of whether there *is* a right kind, or whether what's right is simply *chacun à son goût.* That is, one begins by considering the sorts of questions that have been raised here. I'm not ready to say what the answers are. What I'm saying is that these should be taken up as legitimate questions. Just as such normative questions have now been raised within the natural sciences, following the recognition of the social, military, and political efficacy of theoretical science in its applications, so too in a science which is by its very nature an applied science—in the science of development you also have to raise these questions. You can't ignore them. That doesn't mean you give up autonomous theoretical work, observation or historical analysis. But it means that the framework within which these inquiries are pursued can't avoid these normative questions. That's the ''good'' side to come down on, methodologically.

KAGAN: Just one question: Do you permit the possibility that the answer will be No, we don't know how children should develop?

WARTOFSKY: I would permit that answer as an admission of ignorance, but not as a conclusion. To say that we don't know how they should develop doesn't yet answer the question of how should they develop. Maybe we don't know how they *do* develop, but we do have many different ideas about how they *should* develop. The question is, can we be self-critically articulate and responsible in discussing *that very question* as part of the project of developmental psychology?

KAGAN: By what criteria do we know how they should develop?

WARTOFSKY: If I were to begin answering you, I would then be entering into that very discussion itself. What I am saying is that your asking that question and my answering it should be a proper part of the field of developmental psychology, and that it isn't yet.

GILLIGAN: Isn't it inescapable because if we trace cognitive development, as Jerry Bruner said yesterday, by tracing the growth of mathematical-logical thinking, we are by doing that, according to you, influencing the development.

WARTOFSKY: Of course.

GILLIGAN: Even though we might not say we take a position that this is the best form of development—cognition or anything else—[we do so by] the very fact that that's what we study rather than artistic thinking.

WARTOFSKY: I was touched, and I guess my view of Piaget clarified yesterday, by the remark that Piaget wasn't making the kind of claim that some Piagetians seem to make, namely that child development is essentially ''cognitive,'' if by ''cognitive'' we mean what some leading French theorists have decided cognition is, in their culture: namely, that it's the unfolding of mathematical rationality, as the essence of cognition.

GILLIGAN: You think he's responsible then?

WARTOFSKY: He's responsible in some ways. Yesterday's remark, quoting Piaget, suggests that he had a broader view of cognition than I described. On the other hand, although you may have heard him say that many times, I don't think it's clear from his work. Nor is it clear if one studies the historical development of this thought, because he's very much in the tradition that takes mathematical-scientific thought—the ''adult scientific world-view''— as the essence and end of cognitive development. Now, Piaget may say, ''Well, I'm not really making this claim.'' But the body of his work, which is the leading body of work in developmental and genetic epistemology and in developmental psychology as well, seems to indicate that that's what we should mean by intelligence, or by cognition for that matter. I'm not willing to say that one shouldn't focus on this form of cognition; but one should also focus on moral and aesthetic development. Now, I think they are all cognitive. I'm not ready to give up ''cognitive'' activities, ''cognitive'' practices to intellectual-scientific models of thought alone. Although Piaget certainly talked about moral judgment, and there is, in the work on imagery, a concern with pictorial representation and symbolism in Piaget, nevertheless these are all subordinated, in the great tradition of French philosophical-scientific thought, to the mathematical, rational paradigm, in terms of stages of what's "higher" and what's "lower." But then Piaget does a very funny thing. He waffles very often between a normative and a descriptive approach to this question. He says, in effect, that the norm and telos of child development, cognitively, is the adult scientific world-view. Now Piaget states, in *Mechanisms of Perception,* and in other places, that he is not claiming that the "adult scientific world-view" that we now have is the right and final one. He is just saying that it's the best one we have. (He's like Quine in this respect.) So Piaget says, it's not for me to decide normatively whether that's the truth or the best view. "I leave that question," he says, "to the sociologists of science, the philosophers of science, the historians of science."

On the other hand, if you take this theory, especially as it is more systematically presented in *Biologie et Connaissance,* as an account of how cognition is the further evolution of the originally instinctual forms of animal behavior, then what is the grand schema of development here? It doesn't branch off into moral, aesthetic and practico- this, that, or the other. It's not simply a factual description of what the adult scientific world view happens to have become historically, but rather turns out to be an orthogenetic, and hence normative, account of cognitive development culminating in logico-mathematical rationality as its "highest" achievement. But in fact, human cognitive development *does* take place in history (though not only in the history of scientific thought), and where else should one look for its norms, therefore? Now I find that a very difficult question to deal with because I don't think there is any other place to look except immanently in the historical development of human thought and praxis. I don't think we have a place to stand from which we can look at that from the outside and think, "Oh well, that's only a limited thing, just world history." From a God-like point of view that's just a small episode in cosmic history. That's the only place we have to work from, so I think that the norms have to be reconstructed immanently from within this history, and I find that a very difficult question.

BRUNER: You made the remark about the cultural-historical Marxist point of view to the effect that one uses these external representations, so to speak, for the ends of creating minds and shaping minds, and then you went on to say that one uses them consciously and that rather surprised me. Would you expand on that a little because I was very surprised that you introduced the notion of consciousness there. There is some of that in Marx but certainly in a lot of the neo-Marxists, the cultural-historical ones, that has certainly passed out now—the notion of consciousness . . .

WARTOFSKY: I wasn't aware of that.

KAPLAN: A Cartesian notion of consciousness may have passed out.

WARTOFSKY: Oh, yes. When I said that they consciously take these external representations to be . . . Something can't be a representation unless it is taken to be one. Anything can be taken to be a representation of anything else. These may be taken as two axioms. What gets taken to be a representation is a function of practice, history, culture, and any number of other constraints. But this is in keeping with some of the things that were said (and by you as well). I take the human, social, cognitive consciousness not simply to be *represented* "out there" but to *be,* to exist "out there". When I say what human consciousness is, I don't simply mean what's under the skin or "in the head." I mean [pointing to artifacts] this is human consciousness, this is human consciousness, so is this . . .

BRUNER: Oh, in the sense of objective meaning.

WARTOFSKY: In a sense, yes: the consciousness objectifies itself. This is the way in which it becomes possible for us to become *self*-conscious, that is, to lay the foundation for something which goes beyond animal consciousness in which this self-consciousness doesn't yet arise or arises only incipiently. So that's why I take the production and use of artifacts and language to be the crucial move in the transition from what you might call animal consciousness to human self-consciousness, by means of the capacity to make and use things in a representational or symbolic way.

BRUNER: It's an interesting point. If I can add just one little thing—you remember in Ryle's *Concept of Mind* when he asks where is the mind. He comments on the fact that the mind is in the lorry driver's hand, it's in the screwdriver of the skilled craftsman—that same notion of objectification in the activity and the tools that make possible the use of mind.

WARTOFSKY: But what develops on the basis of this—and here I'm going to borrow from everybody, from Janet, Piaget, Vygotsky and all the other people who consciously or unconsciously adopted the Hegelian theory of consciousness—what happens as a result of the use of this external, practical representational activity is the possibility for the internalization of these modes of representation, the possibility of *reflective* consciousness. To put it very baldly, there is no internal representation possible until there is external representation practiced as a significant feature of a mode of life, "no mentation without representation," so to speak. So, although animals do have incipient and partial use of what you might call proto-symbolic modes of representation—recognition of things as standing for other things and even the creation of some representation forms—markings, and so forth—this is not the primary feature of the species life of any animal. It's at most a subsidiary or very unimportant feature. For human beings culture as the creation of representation artifacts, of meanings embodied in the use and production of artifacts, of language, becomes the crucial identifying species characteristic. That's a much larger thesis than I can corroborate here.

BERNSTEIN: In some ways I am enormously sympathetic with what you are saying, and many people want to believe what you're saying. The question is whether we can. There's an interesting way in which your historical sketch works. One can see so clearly how the fourth stage, which you called the Dadaist, the anarchistic, emerges out of the third stage. For me, and I would think for you, it poses some very difficult questions, particularly when you said that all we can do is look at what is immanent. Look at the leap you make to the end. It's still very much committed to the third model in which there is the belief that it may be more complicated, it may be trickier than we imagine, but with understanding can develop a kind of positive construction. Now, one way of reading the fourth stage model is that the facts seem to belie that. Let me take just one example. One way of interpreting Foucault's work is: Let's look at the interesting dynamic that you talk about; what has been the history of it? The history has been *not* that understanding leads to emancipation, but to a kind of control. There is an inversion in which the so-called human disciplines become a line of furthering the disciplinary society.

WARTOFSKY:. I read it differently. I'm not an anarchist or a Dadaist or a pessimist about this. I do think there has been an increase in human self-awareness and scientific knowledge. I think anybody who denies that is simply doing so from a rather narrow, ideological point of view. We know more than we did, we know better than we did, and we can do more with it than we were able to do in the past. If we don't, that's Rousseau's conundrum: ''Man is born free, yet he is everywhere in chains.'' If we don't do better than we have in the past, why don't we? The question is: If we have developed these capacities, how come they are being used in such a way that they seem to undercut the very liberation or development of human possibilities they seem to exhibit? The fourth anti-developmental theory of development itself is pregnant with suggestions for where to go next. It's not only Foucault. It's Kuhn, it's the whole move of deconstruction, and that's why these people feel so great an affinity for each other.

BRUNER: They do produce that Cartesian panic, even in themselves.

WARTOFSKY: Well, the result of Cartesian panic was Cartesianism. That was his way of coming to terms with the panic. Hume was much more at home in the world than was Descartes. He didn't have to grab hold of certainty the way Descartes did, to hold things down. Now we have seen through the myth of unilinear progress through history, the myth of constant accretion, of inevitable progress, of the Hegelian unfolding of the world spirit. We have seen through that because, on closer analysis, it just ain't so. What is so, however? One view is that it's just one damn thing after another and no way to hold them together. So why don't we just live with that or recognize self-consciously that the myths that we create ain't so—that they *are* myths that we simply create to make ourselves feel better? "Truth" is that kind of a myth, in Nietzche's view. It's an instrumentality by means of which we calm our panic. Now, if you're at that stage of skepticism, then I think you are at the incipient stage of reformulating the notion of development in a much more sophisticated and subtle way, informed now by the kind of empirical, historical, critical study of what is actually going on, so that you can't bluff, you can't impose an ideological schema on a world which you know doesn't fit it. So, I think it's a very fruitful period; but my reading of it isn't one which is quite as pessimistic or despairing or as nihilistic as—you mentioned the names. They all end up in very much the same place and therefore it almost makes you think there is a Zeitgeist—Foucault and Kuhn and Rorty and MacIntyre and Derrida . . .

BRUNER: Not quite, I don't think . . .

WARTOFSKY: No, no. I'm not claiming that they all say the same thing. But I am saying that there is a sense in which these all are comparable responses to the breakdown of the third stage, so to speak.

BERNSTEIN: Part of the question I think you evaded. You put it this way. Yes it is true that there is false consciousness. It is true that we thought that we've understood and then it's turned out that we haven't understood. But what is that? That's a challenge for further understanding, and when we do come to a kind of deeper understanding there is always the real possibility of a kind of direction, some type of directionality necessary to human life. Critical discourse can be efficacious. The part of the challenge that I wanted you to face is that though that is something which is extraordinarily deep in the whole tradition of Western thinking, there are now grounds to be very skeptical of the truth of the essential premise, which is crucial to where you want to end up and, in some ways, where I want to end up. You follow me?

WARTOFSKY: Yes, I do follow you and I feel the strain. In a sense I feel myself pushed out very far on a limb and embattled by this skepticism. But finding out that what we thought just ain't so is very astringent—it's a condition for not permitting yourself to go along with what is no longer adequate. It's the overcoming of a false consciousness or the recognition of ignorance in place of what was previously a claim to knowledge; and that to me is intellectually or humanly progressive.

KAPLAN: I'm not quite sure where I read a dispute between Foucault and Derrida where Foucault claims that Derrida is trying to be the ultimate judge despite the fact that he questions such a possibility. It's an interesting kind of phenomenon because there is an implication there of a demand for certain kinds of standards. I think that is ingredient amongst the anarchists.

WARTOFSKY: There is a phrase of Feuerbach's which I like. He says criticism is easy; construction is very, very hard.

7 General Discussion

FRANKLIN: For this discussion the panelists have given us questions, but they are in no way to limit the discussion. We will entertain questions and comments from the audience, and, in that spirit, we will begin with a question that's not on our list.

BRUNER: I want to go back to the two modes of orientation—the caring and the excelling. I wanted to pose to Carol that there are ways in which society highlights one of those values as compared to the other. It gives an illustration of the way in which a culture creates a kind of self, the notion of man being self-creating as well as culture-creating.

Everything I know about the early development of language tells me that there is early sensitivity to the distinctions that mark these modes. One is sharply marked and the other is left as the residual. If you look at semantic development, the distinctions that are early learned are: active versus passive, strong versus weak, and good versus bad. Active and strong and good go together from the point of view of semantic differential. Now, out of the study of pidgin [English] you find that the first things that get put into the new language are causative versus non-causative—the active kind of doing, causing things to happen, which is quite different from the waiting and caring and letting come to you; punctual versus non-punctual; punctual refers to events that take place Zap, "I slapped the table,"—non-punctual, "I wait for my cousin to come home so that I can give him/her supper." The language gets built in very early on.

Next, you begin to see a technology as you grow up. If you note the technologies of caring as compared to the technologies of excelling, you will notice that mostly we move toward capital intensiveness in those things that have to do with domination. We have cars that go fast, Archimedean levers that lift lots of weight, and so on. It has only been in recent years that we've looked at the more caring, containing types of things—sleeping arrangements, ways of giving comfort—the soft technology of care doesn't get capital intensity. There are a lot of ways that it can be capital intensive; for example, providing child care, putting money into it, is like that.

Now, on the social side, for example, for a little boy being mindful of the kinds of thoughts little girls have is regarded as terribly sissy or something of that sort. I don't remember having asked a little girl, "Why don't you like baseball as much as I do?" On the other hand, I can remember girls asking boys questions of the sort, "Why are you interested in so and so?" The idea of the intra-subjective gets tabooed. Those earlier anthropologists, Mauss and Hertz, talk about the fact that one of the things characteristic of taboo is that you build in a professional incapacity. The example in that great tradition is the left hand. The left hand can do lots of things that we won't allow it to do because it stands for sinistrality, bastardy, a sort of womanliness, and so on. I've just read an autobiography of Patrick White, the Australian Nobel laureat in literature, *In a Flawed Glass*. He talks about his recognition of his homosexuality when he was entering his teenage period. Nobody wanted to hear anything from him about the way he saw things unless it conformed with the idea that when you were in London you went to Lords to see a cricket match with your father. Other preferences were regarded as so bizarre that they were never processed. They are expunged from consciousness in a way.

Lionel Trilling made a point about the distinction [between] sincerity and authenticity: As you move toward a more technical, a more bureaucratic society, in place of having authenticity, this reciprocity and care, you move toward a kind of simulacrum of it, which is sincerity. You wear the right kind of clothes and say the right kind of things. People don't know anything about your background. Under those circumstances, the kind of thing people would directly learn about care by living in a Gemeinschaft rather than Gesellschaft also gets suppressed.

I want to make a funny final remark. Plato, in *The Republic,* has a long thing about how you should ban artists from the Republic. The justification is that they are disorderly, impulsive; they will set people to thinking non-rationally. I think what Plato really meant is that he would have liked to get rid of women in the Republic altogether, but you couldn't do that because that would interfere with the procreative function. So what he did was to get rid of artists instead. I want to see much more investigation carried out jointly by anthropologists and psychologists [to] find out how we impose this business of being self-made and creating our own environments, control people or punish them, in Foucault's sense, by regulating the range in which their cognitive process can operate.

KAGAN: This is an addition to Jerry's comment. Carol, we're changing what you said. I heard you as saying that the two ways of interacting with others are to connect or to dominate. It would be a mistake if we enlarged that category to include autonomy, achievement, and excellence. Most of the middle-class children I know excel in order to get nurture from their parents. It is a way to stay connected. Comment on this because I heard you saying the power voice can be heard not for any malicious end but because hierarchy is one way to interact. I'm asking: Do you want us to include autonomy and achievement? I hope your answer is no.

GILLIGAN: I really appreciate your comment. The answer is no to that. What I was trying to do was to counter the notion that one mode is a mode of relationship and the other, of non-relationship. I was trying to say that there are two forms of relationship that must be differentiated. One is hierarchical or its correction. Here is where the notion of autonomy comes in, that is, equality contract: constraint or cooperation between two autonomous people who agree on a set of rules that they will live by. Piaget observes, and I think very correctly, that out of this social dimension comes the idea of justice. In other words, the experience of inequality, the insight into the possibility of equality, autonomy, gives rise to the idea of justice as an ideal. What I am saying is there is another dimension of relationship, where the connection is not either to constrain or to contract agreement, but, through want of a better word, interdependence. The two dimensions are not symmetrical because one is either-or, inequality-equality; the model of development is one of replacement. How does interdependence develop? You have to have a different model of development to imagine it because it's additive; interdependence elaborates.

KAGAN: I don't think this is nitpicking, Carol, but I'm bothered by your use of justice. It seems to me there's a justice that flows from my connections. I heard you saying that the other appeal to justice is to an impersonal proposition; that is, what you call the male voice. The voice you call female is concerned with justice, but its justice comes out of our relationship, my obligation to you—that's a matter of justice.

GILLIGAN: The argument becomes semantic at this point. The one appeals to abstract rules, principles, and so forth; the other appeal is, "You should respond to me." Attend to me, know me, respond to me, and I should do that to you—I would like to keep the word justice out of this because justice starts with a premise of similarity, equal respect. I don't need to see you as the same as me. In fact, to know you I must undertake a whole realm of activities—listening to you, talking to you, asking all the questions. A "journey of discovery" is what I would call it: to focus on the other, to get to know the other so that you can respond to the other, and then, in adolescence, turn that mode of discovery toward the self.

KAPLAN: Can I pursue that a little? I remember Marx saying that there are occasions where you don't want to talk to the other, you don't want to listen to the other person. Very often faculty say, "Now we will listen to the students, and they will give us some input," and then we will ignore them. There are a number of forms of interdependence. Right? Are there any privileged forms, for you, of interdependence?

GILLIGAN: The question that I would have added to the list if I had thought of it earlier is, "Does justice always dominate care?" Care depends on people staying there. One person can leave and that's why there is a vulnerability to that. If you think of the implications of nuclear power and so forth, the actions of one group on this planet now leave no place of escape for other people. In the past you could go live somewhere else. This option has been cut off. Has that fundamentally changed something so that you have to start thinking about not how to leave but how to stay?

KAPLAN: But that still says it has been cut off, a statement of fact; it has now been cut off.

GILLIGAN: I'm not a seer into the future. I don't know if we'll go live on other planets.

KAPLAN: No, I'm asking you to be a seer into possibilities, not into the future.

GILLIGAN: The possibility that interests me and we come back to my initial question: Does justice always dominate care?

BRUNER: *Does* it do it or *must* it?

GILLIGAN: That's right. It has in the past and always silenced that voice. It has a kind of hard time being heard.

KAGAN: Well, affirmative action may represent it even though it is not as successful as we may want. That's where care dominated justice.

GILLIGAN: Well, that's a good example. Really in direct conflict with each other.

KAPLAN: I don't know whether this is germane but I keep thinking of that supposed evolutionary transition from status law to contract law, recognition of who the other people are as opposed to impersonal principles. Are you advocating in some way, as a value, the return to whatever the contemporary interpretation would be of status [law]?

GILLIGAN: But Bernie, you've come right back: There are two alternatives, hierarchy or contract; which do you want? I'm trying to say there is a third alternative. The autonomous person can choose to care.

KAPLAN: I don't know if Marx wanted to pick it up.

WARTOFSKY: Suppose you have an idea of caring as a relation which has been suppressed. Isn't the fact that it is suppressed an objective matter of fact?

Maybe conditions are such that it simply doesn't have a place in the dominant relationships that characterize the given society. I think this is very important because if you don't ask the question in that way, then you set up communities of caring individuals who persist in the pores of society, in little "islands of civility," to borrow a phrase (from MacIntyre), instead of saying what conditions are necessary for this other voice to realize itself more broadly, and asking how to go about creating the conditions under which this would be possible.

The interesting thing is the historical framework within which this has been analyzed. In the *Grundrisse,* Marx describes pre-capitalist (e.g., feudal) forms of social relations which are particularistic, personal, having to do with obligations of status and role, where there is mutual dependency of lord on serf and serf on lord and of everybody on everybody else. Then you get this sharp break, with the development of commodity production and of wage labor, where any person can be substituted for any other one in the social relations of capitalist production. The condition of equality is that we are all equal in the claims that we can make against each other. Therefore, we are all intersubstitutable in a court of law or in the marketplace. One of the reactions to the excesses of this abstract depersonalized equality was the backward-looking, romantic medievalism which idealized the organic community: "Let's return to the values of the medieval community, to the particularistic personal caring, where the serf knew that his master was going to take good care of him, instead of throwing him on a labor market to shift for himself." These different emphases are historically contingent and variable. The question is, "Well, does that mean our emphasis on the value of caring is not good, because it means we're returning to feudalism?" Obviously not.

There is one other point. The classical Hegelian model of domination is the so-called master-slave analogy. That relation of domination is the relation of necessary interdependence. The master can't be a master unless he has a slave, and the slave can't be a slave except in relation to a master. They are interdefined, interdependent; they're bound to each other in the relation of domination and subordination. So there *is* an interdependence, but not the kind one would want. Interdependence as such is not the value, but an interdependence of mutual equality, which then introduces into the interdependence the elements of equality and justice which are taken from the other more abstract side.

BERNSTEIN: It does seem to me semantic in the sense that there is a certain verbal confusion. When you speak about justice, equality, and so forth, you're really speaking about a kind of modern liberal enlightenment conception. I think it's your more interesting hypothesis that the two voices are really total perspectives in which all the key terms take on slightly different meanings. Any attempt to take a set of terms as privileged is working against your main and more interesting point. It is more interesting because your attempt to do justice to the distinctiveness of these voices is the way in which, from the other side, there is always an encoding or translation: "Oh, I understand what you mean but this is where it fits."

GILLIGAN: That's very good. I really appreciate it.

KAPLAN: Then you are dealing almost with two commensurate systems.

BERNSTEIN: This is where Carol is still thinking about this issue in the sense of "Okay, is it really incommensurate?" Look at the ways you can go: You can say that it is incommensurate; that maybe there is some type of overcoming; or that, even, it might be tragic in the sense that it cannot be reconciled. I think you are still thinking out for yourself exactly how they can be related.

KAGAN: Let's be—as we have been for two days—dynamic and historical, not static. It is only incommensurate for a moment. One can view this issue historically, as we have. But let us view it psychologically. Two strangers meet. In that initial encounter we ask, is the primary concern who will dominate, or is the primary concern, will we accept one another?

I agree that women are more likely to assume the latter stance. But, we know men will bond as well as compete. As a relationship develops the voices are not incommensurate.

BERNSTEIN: Here's where I think you are being historical. Whether the whole set of forces in our society that constantly reinforces what she is calling the male model is of such a nature that even though you hear the other things, institutionally it gets relegated to what Marx calls the margins.

KAPLAN: Marginally, to Jerry Kagan, I think we tend to talk as though psychological processes are ahistorical.

I think there is a tendency to say that we can take these relationships outside of the socio-historical context and talk about psychologically resolving them as though there was some kind of psychological invariant over all. We can raise the question about the variability of the cultural world in different historical circumstances. Psychological categories are taken to be invariant as though we had once and for all discovered them.

[Many voices ask to come to Jerry Kagan's defense]

WARTOFSKY: There might not be any kind of psychological essence being expressed here, but there may be some trans-historical invariances of a certain sort. The dualities being expressed here, which Jerry Bruner commented on in language and which came up in Carol's description of the alternative kinds of social relations, bear looking at as a set of very pervasive invariants of this sort. It begins with Pythagoras, with the "one" and the "two," the numerical metaphors of unity and duality: the male and the female. The male is one—*light, good, rational, unified* (and I forget what else goes in Pythagoras' "male" column). The female column is *dark, irrational, divisive,* and so forth. And the "two" is obviously the bad one, the inferior one. And why "two?" Because "one" is not yet a number; "one" is the principle from which number comes, the generator of number. "Two" is the first number therefore. But with "two," with "number," you no longer have perfection, or simple unity, but rather multiplicity, change, corruption and mortality. So there is a very old sexual metaphor working here.

Now, suppose you were to apply this dualistic schema to some kind of typology of social relations of different sorts that may have different expressions. Suppose you wanted a developmental theory of sociality, a theory of what kinds of social relations there are, in order to then investigate which ones you think are developmentally more advanced, or better. Instead of taking historical categories, like *ruling* and *ruled,* or *dominating* and *dominated,* suppose you take more concrete ones—you have *employer-employee, teacher-student, parent-child.* You have, also, the *judger* and the *judged* (which holds for standards of literary criticism as well as for standards of law); you have *buyers* and *sellers;* you have *speakers* and *listeners.* They are not all of one type. In some, there is a hierarchical relationship; in others not.

I was thinking of what Carol was talking about as alternative kinds of relationships. I came up with this in teaching a course in the philosophy of medicine. The doctor-patient relation has built into it the active/passive attitude. The patient is acted on and the doctor is the agent who does the acting. Here you have the causative/non-causative, active/passive, strong/weak semantic relations. What are the conceivable permutations on the doctor-patient relationship which either do or do not fall into this pattern? Traditionally, there is the authority relation of domination and subordination based on the authority of knowledge. Doctors know what to do to patients, hence they have authority. The patient comes to the doctor because of dependence on the doctor's cognitive authority, institutionalized in medical practice. That's obviously a relation of domination and subordination.

You have another relation in medical practice which is more a mapping of the liberal notion of market-equality—service for a fee. Here there is an exchange of equivalents. The doctor will give you service which is an equivalent in the exchange in value for a fee. So you have a buyer and seller, i.e., the traditional model of contract-relations or of market-relations. Both are free agents who voluntarily enter into a relationship with each other in which each takes what the other is giving; each satisfies the other's need. It is a free and equal exchange. So you have that model of the doctor-patient relationship which a number of theorists (usually conservative) have been urging on the profession, namely, that there is no *right* to health care. Health care is a commodity. It is to be gotten for a fee and therefore the seller is free to refuse to sell or to sell to whomever he wants.

Much older in medicine is the tradition of caring. It has always been regarded as going along with medical practice as a curative practice, but it's usually associated most distinctively with nursing, traditionally considered a feminine occupation although historically not. Caring or ministering to needs in the hospital and in the medieval hospice were not predominantly feminine occupations in the older medical context. Caring is still an asymmetrical relationship, not one of equality. There is the carer and the cared for: one gives, the other takes or receives.

Then you have an alternative like the one Carol mentioned, which is becoming more current now as a result of the patients' rights movement and lots of other developments in medicine and politics. In psychiatry, in psychology, and in law, one doesn't say "patient," one says "client." That's a different relationship, purportedly one of cooperation towards a mutual end where each one is informing the other or helping the other to achieve something they are both committed to. Therefore, this is viewed as a cooperative relation in which the responsibility is equally shared, though differentiated. The shared end is still the health or well-being of the "client," however, and not of the health professional.

GILLIGAN: Let me extend your example. There's a nice article by Searles called "The Patient as Therapist to his Analyst." Let's assume you have a theory of psychopathology that it is rendering ineffective the child's efforts to care and to help that [is] partly causative of illness. Then, the therapy: The now grown-up child must experience himself or herself as effective, as someone who can be responsive, caring, nurturant. That means that you have a doctor-patient relationship—called counter-transference, illegitimate, and so forth, on the part of the doctor—to feel cared for by the patient. It will disappear with the process of cure. What's interesting is that they are not reductive. The three dimensions that you list in the doctor-patient relationship seem to me all to exist in that relationship.

WARTOFSKY: Yes, they are not mutually exclusive.

GILLIGAN: It's important, in the sense of Dick's comment, too, to see how the same words, as they move from one dimension to the other, will take on different connotations.

BERNSTEIN: It's not really to this issue, but I feel a certain injustice has been done to Jerry Kagan and I want to come to his defense. Perhaps it is . . .

WARTOFSKY: A caring person, Dick.

BERNSTEIN: No, I just want justice. [Laughter]

I think that there are two forms of reductivism which we would all agree are just absolutely wrong. [One] form of reductivism has the presumption that we now know enough about the human body or biology to be able to read off global facts about development. Despite the fact that there are presumably intelligent [people] who say it, they are wrong. On the other hand, it seems to be equally wrong, the reductionism that would like to forget the fact that we have bodies. The middle area is an area about which we are tremendously ignorant. We really do not know to what extent there are biological constraints of various kinds. We simply do not know although many people, in the spirit of Jerry, say it is a perfectly legitimate and important enterprise to try and see as far as we can go to come up with it. I think that's really the heart of what you are saying, so I'd like to get out of those either/ors. It seems to me pernicious that we forget that we're biological, that we have bodies, and that in some sense which we have not yet clearly determined, it sets constraints on all the interesting issues—whether we're talking about linguistic development, cognitive development, moral development. That's my apologia, in the classical sense, for what you really want to hold out for.

KAGAN: That's right, and well stated.

AUDIENCE MEMBER: I felt the same way. I wanted to come to Jerry Kagan's defense because I think certain things are true for all human beings. If you talk about critical periods, for example, you would probably do better in the beginning to work with physical activities. It occurred to me earlier, when so much emphasis was put on the historical conditions, that, at the end of the last century there were lots of people who were basically against it—such as Helmholtz or William James, who held ideas that were much closer to what you were proposing. [Is there] any way of taking off from that?

KAGAN: I would like to say one thing related to Bernie's question to me—he didn't use this predicate—"Can you parse phenomena?" I interpreted Bernie as implying one cannot parse phenomena, and I disagree. Example: Five years ago there was a hurricane off a reef in Jamaica and there was elimination of some species and growth of other species in less than 2 years. Even though we know historical forces operating for millenia formed the island, one can also say that the hurricane caused a distinct disruption of certain species. When I said to Carol that, in the interpersonal realm, males react one way, females another, you [Bernie] said to me, "Wait a minute. There is historical conditioning."

KAPLAN: No. I was talking about historical conditioning of the categories of the mind. Just like there is historical conditioning of the categories of what we take to be non-mind. See, I wanted to defend you also. [Laughter] Let me just say this. This is partly directed toward Dick. Yes, we may find there are *present* biological constraints. You also have to think of the possibility that what are taken to be biological constraints . . .

BERNSTEIN: Of course. There is no issue on this.

KAPLAN: I thought there was no issue, but I just wanted to be sure.

FRANKLIN: Some of the points in this most recent part of the discussion lead us directly to one of the questions on the participants' list:

"On the one hand, several participants have expressed skepticism and caution about the value presuppositions of theories of development—especially concerning how value presuppositions are to be 'justified' or 'warranted.' But on the other hand, there has been the suggestion that there are (or may be) universal features of human development (including moral and social development) which can be discovered by psychological inquiry. How does one reconcile the tentativeness (and/or confusion) about the plurality of value presuppositions with empirical claims to universality?"

KAGAN: I want to make one point briefly. I don't know why I think of Bernie when I think of this question. We need not demand immaculate knowledge. We have to accept uncertainty and imperfection in all knowledge. Therefore, we acknowledge that our presuppositions influence our inquiry, but that doesn't mean we stop psychological inquiry. As I heard you this morning, it sounded as if you were saying "immaculate knowledge or none." I hope you weren't.

KAPLAN: Oh, no. Let me clarify what I'm saying. If you say there is imperfection, I take it you have some vague glimmering, even though it's not achieved or achievable, of what you mean by perfection.

KAGAN: It's an ideal.

KAPLAN: That's what I'm saying. I take it for granted. In no case will there be perfection.

GILLIGAN: Aristotle, in the ethics, described the youthful character in ways that almost directly parallel Anna Freud, Erik Erikson and Peter Blos' description of adolescence. If you read Aristotle's description to a psychology class and asked who said it, they will tell you Anna Freud or someone like that because they observed the same things—for example, the swinging between extremes, the devotion or passion for ideals, etc. Do we say it's because they shared the same presuppositions that they saw the same aspects at the time, or is there something about adolescence that no matter whether you look in ancient Greece or in Vienna . . .

WARTOFSKY: If I may try a double answer to that. In one of his better known aphorisms, Whitehead once said that the whole history of philosophy was a series of footnotes to Plato. What we call the Western tradition (I like to remind my students that what we call Western philosophy or Western thought started in the eastern end of the Mediteranean on the Asian continent, in what is now Turkey) [Laughter] but in the Western tradition, there is a kind of causal, social, historical, ideational continuity. It wouldn't be entirely amiss to say that the characterization of adolescence in what was, after all, for its time an extraordinarily urban culture, is not so far, in context, from what we now know, and it was the shaping conception and model from which a great deal of Western civilization in its social forms developed.

Suppose there is an historical invariance there. It's an open question whether that universality is to be attributed to the period of physiological or emotional growing pains where everything is out of whack. One may say: How are you going to be stable when your nervous system and your musculature and your endocrine system are undergoing such radical transformations? Or maybe it's a function of a particular, relatively invariant, but highly differentiated continuum in the cultural sense. The real test would be presumably to do cross-cultural, cross-historical studies to see whether there is such a thing as adolescence in very different cultures. Then you're into the kind of (Michael) Cole-(Sylvia) Scribner problem. How do you bring to the cross-cultural study something which isn't going to infect it with the very categorical scheme which you are testing cross-culturally? One of the striking intellectual discoveries I made as an adolescent was in reading Frazer's *Golden Bough:* In Oceanic cultures, as in others, during the period of menstruation, women were not allowed either to come in contact with the ground, or with crops, or with growing things, because they would kill them off or make them infertile, because they were (in a word which I knew from my grandmother) "tume"; they were unclean. I said, "My God, in Polynesia too?" [Laughter] I thought it was only my grandmother, who at a certain time in the month—which I didn't understand then—wouldn't give things to my grandfather directly but would put them on the table for him to pick up, and wouldn't water the plants. Now in Polynesia, they put the menstruating women in huts so that they wouldn't be touching the soil to make it unclean. Under what conditions does that particular thing occur? Is there cultural transmission we don't know about or is there something culturally analogous to what happens in so-called convergent evolution, where you get similar forms in different contexts where there is no genetic transmission at all?

That's a research question. I don't think it can be settled a priori. So, when I was being critical yesterday of what Jerry [Kagan] was saying and he said, "Well, you are just disagreeing with me," what I was disagreeing about was that particular jump. What you seemed to be saying was that one can make the jump, should it be biological explanation of some of these behavioral or characterological or moral things. I think we agree that both of those have to be examined. There is one other example from the same source: My grandmother obviously had a great influence on my philosophical life because I didn't know until much later, when I had read Plato, that she was a Platonist. She used to explain to me that this little indentation that we all have here under our noses comes about because at the moment of birth the angel does this to you [flicks upper lip] and makes you forget everything you knew before you were born. Now this is the Platonic theory of *anamnesis*. This was probably a very, very deep folk myth which Plato expressed in one way and somehow (probably through Alexander's conquests in the Middle East) got passed on to my grandmother's ancestors. That kind of parallelism could have socio-historical or cultural explanations just as well as some roots in biological contingencies of the other sort.

GILLIGAN: Let me just add one thing. It always concerns me when the explanation is either biological or cultural-historical. How about psychological?

WARTOFSKY: I sort of include that in the cultural-historical.

BERNSTEIN: Right. There are other kinds of invariance. I mean, you have translated that issue of invariance into biology.

WARTOFSKY: I tend to think of it that way because biology is the pervasive mode for that kind of an argument. But Jerry Kagan put it in two different ways yesterday and I conflated them. When he was talking about emotional primitives, he was not talking biologically, and I took him to be speaking biologically.

KAGAN: Right, nouns are mastered before verbs in the first hundred words. Is that a psychological universal or biological universal?

BRUNER: This is all becoming terribly familiar because this is exactly the discussion that goes on in linguistics, and it's never got anywhere. Let me give you a few examples. You have diffusionism, you have parallel invention, you have the notion of nativism. I really want to say let's see if we can formulate a Treaty of Westphalia to bring this religious war to an end.

It may even be that Jung was right. There is even a thing like a set of human plights which seem to be inevitable. Everybody cannot have an equal supply when things are in short supply. Under those circumstances you are bound to get into certain kinds of situations that create language to go with it, social forms to go with it. It's conceivable that the greatest riches come from finding instances in which you do have certain native predispositions, which as anthropologists have been saying now for two decades, are exploited by the culture because they are more easily come by. Why should a culture take something which is non-natural and try to convert it into a convention? It's crazy. And so, I don't think we really need argument. It's only when one person makes an imperial claim with respect to their way of doing it that it really starts getting boring as it has become boring in linguistics now for at least two centuries.

FRANKLIN: I understood this question not to be "Are there universals and if so what are they and are they biologically based?" but to be a meta-theoretical question.

BERNSTEIN: In part it was. It was prompted by the way in which you [Bruner] set up your paper yesterday. Because you made your strict distinction and then you made the claim that there can't be a theory of development without values. One interpretation of what you are saying would lead us to think that the value presuppositions of a theory of development are always affecting that theory in such a way that you could never really get at certain universal characteristics.

BRUNER: I would still hold that to be the essential, the tragic question of epistemology. I still think that we are noumena . . . impenetrable.

BERNSTEIN: We have to make a dis-analogy here. For example, with all that we have learned about fallibilism in science and different paradigms, there is implicit in the whole logic of the natural scientific models a claim to universality that recognizes its fallibility. The issue is not theory dependence, context dependence, and so forth. When you make the radical move to the necessity yet in some ways to the non-justifiability of certain value presuppositions, that makes it more serious: whether you can come up with a theory of development which is going to have the characteristics you find in certain natural sciences or that Jerry Kagan does believe you can find even in theories of development.

WARTOFSKY: I'd like to stand above the battle, for the moment, between the imperial claims of alternative paradigms or theories of this sort. Granting that it gets boring when it becomes formalistic, I'd like to make the claim that taking a kind of historicized, pragmatic approach to it is not only a necessary but a useful thing to do. That has to do with the complementarity that is built into theoretical development. It is very, very good that Descartes made the kinds of imperial claims he did for a universal rationality, for the necessity of certain truths, and so forth. In the context of the views that he was criticizing, it served to open up whole areas of research and interpretation which otherwise wouldn't have been developed.

BRUNER: The radical claim of Chomsky about nativism had the same effect.

WARTOFSKY: Exactly, and you can make the same claim for reductionism in the sciences. It has been the most powerful heuristic for the last three hundred years, first in physics and now in biology. It has been very productive in terms of research and discovery. Nevertheless, just as interesting, the argument against reductionism has also had heuristically good effects in the sciences as a corrective. I am proposing a kind of meta-theory that the dialectic of theoretical change often requires an imperial claim as an articulation of the way of doing things which gets you out of the particular bind that the state of the art leaves you in. So when Chomsky made his move toward radical [nativism] . . . I remember asking him many years ago, "Why do you want to use the term *innate ideas?*'' He said, ''To rile the opposition.'' And it did the trick.

That particular tradition has a lot of conceptual payoff to it. And then you discover, well, it doesn't work. You discover when you push it, it doesn't work past a certain point; it begins to break down.

KAPLAN: That's sort of Jung's enantiodromia, ''tuning into the opposite,'' and that I take as a critique of my notion of perfection. You push as far as it will go, like Skinner, only to see when you push it beyond a certain point there is some limitation to it. Then you're obliged to swing over the other way.

WARTOFSKY: It's a kind of opportunism. I hate to say it, but opportunistically it has had a history of profound effects in scientific development . . . that kind of imperial claim making. There is one view in the philosophy of science, Lakatos's version of a theory of research programs which says (to put it very crudely) that all theories are born false. The only principle of choice among theories is whether they lead to productive research activity.

FRANKLIN: I think the next two questions might go together. Here they are:
    ''What are the explicit or tacit value presuppositions within the major theories of psychological development—psychoanalytic theory, social learning theory, Piaget, Werner, Vygotsky? What kinds of ideas about the aims of development are embodied in such a theory?''
    And another question: ''Are there crucial values which *ought* to serve as the presupposition of theories of development, such as freedom, mutualities, which are themselves the proper subject for developmental theory?''

WARTOFSKY: Could I speak to the second one? I'd like to say something about Vygotsky. The Luria book, with its experimental program conceived at Vygotsky's suggestion [*Cognitive Development: Its Cultural and Social Foundations*] published first in the Soviet Union in 1974 and then by Harvard University Press in 1976, reported for the first time publicly the research which they undertook in 1931–33 in Uzbekistan and Kirghizia. They wanted to do field work in what I would now call historical epistemology and had already formulated a program of this sort, partly on psychological grounds alone, partly out of their Marxism. The reason it wasn't published until 1974 was that it was suppressed in 1936. They were studying the cognitive transformations which took place in linguistic or conceptual forms which were concurrent with major social transformations. Here they had a laboratory experiment going on a grand scale. A major social transformation was taking place in Uzbekistan. It was undergoing a rapid and radical transition from an agrarian craft economy to a modern production and exchange economy, with major introduction of money, accounting, machinery, and the need for the kind of abstract conceptual apparatus that goes along with that.

BRUNER: Collectives, too.

WARTOFSKY: Yes, collectives and collective forms of organization. So Luria and Vygotsky were working within the framework of a categorical distinction between the concrete-particular and abstract-universal where the developmental pattern was taken to be from the former to the latter. It wasn't a question of better or worse. There may or may not have been a kind of orthogenetic or historicist connotation there, that you were making progress as you went from one to the other, but you were certainly reporting on historical or social progress and the effects of it on conceptual change or conceptual development. And when they reported their results, the book was suppressed for the interesting reason that it would have the effect of expressing a chauvinistic attitude toward Uzbekistan as being a less developed and backward culture.

Okay, what are the value presuppositions in that kind of research project from two points of view? One is the point of view of the developmental norms, of the move from the concrete to the abstract: that's right in keeping with the traditional notions of the norms of development, whether in Piaget, in Werner, Vygotsky, or in any of the other standard views, despite all the differences among them. And the second one, what are the value presuppositions that go along with the decision that a certain line of research has socially bad effects and therefore was either not to be pursued or not to be published? That's acknowledging or conceding the enormous practical effect of developmental theory and making a decision on that basis.

BRUNER: I had a moral crisis because I reviewed it in *Nature*. That book was absolutely drenched in value presuppositions. It was full of questions like this: "You know there are in the zoo in Minsk white bears and black bears. Do you think there would be any chance of your seeing a white bear in the zoo in Minsk?" And the peasant who hasn't started driving a tractor and keeping accounts in the collective would say things like, "Well, you know, you can't be sure. I've never been to Minsk before." He tried to answer you in terms of things that were close by. From the point of view of a basic Marxist concept, thought matches the context where you live. Since they all lived locally and everything is based on this particular business of whom I'm going to meet today and whom I met yesterday, the answers were perfectly fine. There were lots of indications that these people, given a context, could also think in that abstract way. I found myself coming to the odd conclusion in that review that if they were going to have censorship and one were forced to be a censor, probably at the particular moment in history the censors were right from the point of view of the discouragement that this would bring to the people of Uzbekistan, who now were somehow asked to throw away their history in some odd way. It was an interesting book that was so concerned with linear progress that the whole pattern of thought as being context-sensitive was sort of being wiped out.

GILLIGAN: Since you reviewed the book, you know there is such a beautiful example in it about what you were talking about before. One of their questions stated: There was a three-sided figure; the question was "What is it?" The Uzebekistanis say a "stirrup" and the right answer is a "triangle."

WARTOFSKY: Talk about IQ testing!

BRUNER: Why isn't it a stirrup?

GILLIGAN: I think the question of throwing away your history is a general question that we should talk about here. Does a developmental theory or a notion of human development that equates change with progress commit you to throwing away your history?

BERNSTEIN: Well, let's hear it. That's an interesting question.

GILLIGAN: Put it in the life cycle. One interpretation of adolescence is that adolescents must throw away their history if they are to grow up. I think it's highly questionable, a wrong assumption.

KAPLAN: Of course there's a notion which involves including your history.

GILLIGAN: But if we included history, I would use the metaphor of retelling a story in a different way, from a different perspective. That's a different series of metaphors for development. Then you must include that history in the story rather than judge it and put it aside.

KAPLAN: But you also have to locate it in some way with respect to where you are now because otherwise that is the nostalgia for the past.

GILLIGAN: That's right. But again, you're getting into what are your models for how you order events. The triangle and the stirrup example is wonderful. Is it possible to retain the capacity to see the three-sided figure as both?

KAPLAN: Yes.

GILLIGAN: When you start to see it as a triangle do you begin to lose the particularity and all the associations that go with being a stirrup?

BRUNER: This is the opportunity for becoming abstract. You have to lose your sense of particularity.

GILLIGAN: Is this true?

KAPLAN: Do you lose or do you have to lose? Because you may lose in certain contexts yet that may have to do in some way with, as you suggest, a certain mode of education which involves the presupposition of replacement.

GILLIGAN: And which has been adversely affected by our developmental theories which imply transformation, i.e., that you have to lose.

KAPLAN: I'm very much interested in the question that Marx raised. Remember Connor Cruise O'Brien, I think, in that little book on the morality of scholarship? Should you suppress certain truths? He was really suggesting that you need censorship but that you need censorship in this case because there is a value higher than the value of the pursuit of impersonal truth.

KAGAN: What is that value?

KAPLAN: I just threw it out. I'm not going to answer it. Does anyone want to engage it? Sometimes it has been part of the academic tradition that there is no qualification of the pursuit of what is true. That seems to be a question of value. Do you think that ought to be?

GILLIGAN: You don't attribute such ultimate power to truth.

KAPLAN: But you are saying there is a more important value with regard to persons.

FRANKLIN: You were also, in some of these comments, getting at the question, What if different developmental theories have different ideas in them about the relationship of the past to the present? The view of the relationship of the past to the present is not usually regarded as a value presupposition even when value presuppositions are being discussed. Is that something you want to pursue? Sometimes it helps to refer to specific theories.

BRUNER: I'd like to make just one brief comment on that because I think if you look at Freud, Piaget, and Vygotsky, as in a paper I wrote a few years ago, it's perfectly plain that Freud is principally concerned with the problem of the past and a liberation movement against mistakes made in the past. Piaget, as the kind of structural theorist that he is, is not concerned with the past or the future; he is concerned with the present. It's a totally ahistorical system in which you give your description in terms of the logical structure of the thought processes that go on. And Vygotsky is preoccupied with the future. Vygotsky was interested in the question of how somebody who is more experienced, ahead of another, gives a loan of his consciousness to someone who knows less and somehow allows him to bootstrap up in the future to a level where he has a broader perspective.

AUDIENCE MEMBER: I am thinking back to Carol's presentation yesterday and remembering that I was struck at the time about how, when she spoke about women, she referred to them as "they" rather than "we," and I wondered what's the underlying value in that choice of words.

GILLIGAN: "Objectivity" is the word that comes to mind. I'm trying to recall the specific context and also the grammatical form. I was not part of the research sample that I was talking about, as I remember. I was talking about results of a study of 144 males and females.

AUDIENCE MEMBER: No, I thought at some point you were generalizing and talking about how it is more likely that women will prefer this . . .

FRANKLIN: Aren't you asking the question about—and I don't know whether we should explore this—academic discourse itself? What values it embodies that we may or may not be aware of?

GILLIGAN: I would also think you are asking a second question. Are you asking about how do we think about the relationship between researcher and so-called subject? That word reveals how we think about it.

KAPLAN: I just want to address Jerry's [Bruner] distinction along temporal lines. If anything, Vygotsky, it's not so much the future as the realm of possibility. He's concerned with the past and the present and the future. In some ways Piaget is like the tenseless present.

BRUNER: Yes, that's right. I have done some study of the language of the three of them and my initial intuition is well borne out by linguistic analysis.

WARTOFSKY: I agree that Piaget is not historically oriented, but the genetic structuralism certainly is temporally or developmentally oriented. So, how would you make a distinction between the historical context and the developmental?

BRUNER: This is curious. We always assume that Piaget gives you a temporal account. He doesn't. He gives you a set of simultaneous accounts of stages, and the only mechanism that will give you any temporal travel at all is accommodation and assimilation.

KAGAN: You're absolutely right. Then why does he say he must trace the victory back to the sensorimotor origins?

BRUNER: What do you think?

WARTOFSKY: Because of the logical or ontological dependence of one on the other.

KAGAN: Because he presupposes a connectedness. When he actually starts to write it is all gone.

BRUNER: It's a marvelous mask in a way.

KAGAN: It is a mask, in a way that Freud's writings are not. See, Freud does try to reconstruct.

KAPLAN: Jacques Voneche once told me, in terms of his conversations with Piaget, that Piaget fundamentally denies time. That's probably the influence of Meyerson.

BRUNER: That plus the negative influence of Bergson.

FRANKLIN: Let's look at the last question: "Does a theory of development require the concept of a necessary and inevitable sequence of stages? Is the concept of stages necessarily linked to ideas of progress? What are the value presuppositions of a stage theory?"

KAGAN: I want to change the question and re-phrase it this way: What domains do we think will most require a stage-sequence approach and what domains will not? That would make it a more interesting question.

KAPLAN: A theory of stages or different structures, I might say yes to, but if someone asked me does it require a theory of an inevitable sequence of stages, I would have great reservations. In that sense, I have reservations about Piaget, Kohlberg, and so on.

KAGAN: Expand that.

KAPLAN: There may be logical presuppositions that one stage is a necessary and sufficient condition. Is it a necessary and sufficient condition? That's something you have to find out. It's not something you can presuppose. Nor can you find out, as far as I can see, by examining a finite sample. That's partly the issue of the distinction between universality and generality. In some way you may find it in all the ones you have now seen and it may still not be necessary. You have to show some more stringent criterion of a necessary sequence of stages, and that's why I object, usually, to people talking about a necessary sequence of stages.

BRUNER: I take the radical position that stages are introduced for the convenience of the investigator. If he finds them convenient, let him use them. As far as I'm concerned, they're ontic dumps. They're there to give some kind of reality to something. I find that it has been one of the most anti-dynamic devices introduced into psychology in the last century.

KAPLAN: I agree with you, Jerry. It leads to what I like to call "a disease of encoding."

FRANKLIN: Does anyone want to object to these statements?

BRUNER: I hope so.

BERNSTEIN: Given these two strong statements, I'd like to ask a question that is almost out of innocence. It is one thing to say that various kinds of theories that really do hold for stages or for certain structures may not be convincing. It seems to me another, completely different issue to rule out a priori that possibility.

BRUNER: No, no. Not a priori . . . well, I'll give you an example. You introduce a stage and then you have to introduce notions like vertical and horizontal decalage; you've got all these epicycles, like pre-Copernican astronomy, and by the time you're finished you're really quite out of your mind.

FRANKLIN: I want to ask what the alternative is.

KAGAN: How many would disagree with the statement that there are times in development when the relationship among the basic structures changes? Not in a day, but over a six-month period. Does anyone doubt that?

BRUNER: Yeah.

KAGAN: Okay, good.

FRANKLIN: Would you care to elaborate that? We're supposed to come to a crescendo here.

KAGAN: Jerry, what word should we use for this phenomenon? Between 8 and 12 months of age there is a dramatic enhancement in retrieval memory and appearance of stranger and separation anxiety . . .

BRUNER: Those are marvelous dynamics you're describing. But why should I call that a stage?

KAGAN: There is the appearance of symbolism, and a very reliable increase in selective imitation. Now, those are correlated within a child, and are seen across cultures. Is there an advantage to saying that there is a reorganization that occurs between 8 and 12 months in ontogeny?

KAPLAN: Yes, that would be the ground for talking about a structure.

KAGAN: Okay, fine. But then you're substituting . . .

KAPLAN: No, I'm not saying that I'm opposed to the notion of a structure or a stage. Stage usually has the implication a structure does not.

BRUNER: I would want to make a more stringent statement. You tell me that symbolism is introduced. And immediately, as you say that, such hairs as I have left I want to tear out, because the idea of the introduction of symbolism is madness. It depends on somebody; what they took as a criterion for symbolism. I can show you all sorts of *pars pro toto* behavior during the first month.

KAGAN: The meaning of every description derives from a procedure.

KAPLAN: It's not that I a priori rule out that necessary and sufficient conditions for the second stage come out of the first stage. You may find that, but I wouldn't presuppose that. I don't think Piaget has any basis for arguing for a necessary and sufficient sequence, although I can see that they may function as ideal types.

BRUNER: They are useful.

KAPLAN: They are, and I have no objection to that except when suddenly it is read, as some people have read it, into the ontogenetic sequence.

BRUNER: They talk about operativity as characterizing the operational stages.

FRANKLIN: Will you [Wartofsky] speak to this?

WARTOFSKY: All I want to say is, I am sort of casting about for what might be the conceptual or, if you like, historical roots of the notion of stages. When I think about classical Greek science or philosophy, I don't come up with any stage notions.

BERNSTEIN: Sure you do.

KAPLAN: Aristotle.

BERNSTEIN: And what then is Aristotle's description in the beginning of the metaphysics of the move from sensation . . .

WARTOFSKY: I don't take that to be stages.

BERNSTEIN: Why not?

WARTOFSKY: I take it to be the description of a process in terms of the sequence. If that's all stage means, then it's simply another way of speaking about temporal sequence. There is, in Aristotle, a developmental notion that this is necessary for that, and this comes from that, and so forth. That may be one simple source of it, but I don't feel "stage-y" about that.

On the other hand, when you get into the social practices of initiation, rites of transition, and so forth, and when you get into the dramatization of history, with redemptive history, with the notion of a covenant which then has to be fulfilled at a certain time and in certain ways, then you get the introduction of the notion of historical developmental stages, each of which is inevitable and necessary. In Aristotle there is no inevitability or necessity that an organism will go through all these stages. Only if it develops, will it. It may not. It may be pathological; it may die; it may not make it. When you get a redemptive history you get a notion of necessity in this development—no matter what you do you are fated. Things are inevitable and universal in this respect. Then you get the notion of stages which gets transferred into the sciences, secularized, only when you get a historicization of the sciences—in geology, and with the nebular hypothesis, and so forth. But then the question is, "Is this ontic dumping?" Is this reading a cultural construction into the material, or is this recognizing or discovering an ontological character in the material itself?

KAGAN: Just one comment before Richard speaks. It seems to me that experimental embryology in the late 19th century had a powerful influence on psychology: The changes from blastula to gastrula are stages in a persuasive sense.

BERNSTEIN: I think that there are weaker and stronger notions of stages and I'd like to see if we can get some clarification. So, let's be specific. Kohlberg's theory is a stage theory. They are stages in a certain sense. It's not inevitability. To pass through all of them, that's certainly not the claim, but that they are necessary and sufficient conditions. Now it's one question to ask, "Is this particular theory persuasive, convincing, and so forth?" It seems to be a very different question, and I don't see where you get the right to make the pronouncement, "Is this *type* of theory a theory which is to be . . .

KAPLAN: I was saying just the opposite. I wouldn't assume a priori that it is the theory that constitutes the development, which is what Kohlberg does. I'd say whether it does turn out to be is something to be discovered. He would have to show the necessity and sufficiency, and I don't think he ever does.

BERNSTEIN: Okay, but then you *are* making a specific objection because his claim certainly would be that he has done this. You're claiming it's not sufficient.

KAPLAN: I'd say he has tried to make that claim. I don't see how.

BERNSTEIN: Okay, I really wanted to locate it. When we started asking the question about this, I would have thought—that's why I was a bit surprised by the remarks that you made and that Jerry Bruner made—that it's a very attractive heuristic device to use stages. It is also true that we can look at a whole series of stage theories that have gotten us into all kinds of trouble— you know, Ptolemaic kinds of confusions. But it's an empirical question, and this conceptual device may turn out to be a fruitful device for understanding something about the nature of development.

GILLIGAN: If Jerry wants to call 8 to 12 months of age a stage for these reasons, I don't see any problem with it. It's the value problem that I have with stages like Kohlberg's, and it takes the following form. The minute I say there is a sequence of stages, an invariant order, and a hierarchical transformation, the presumption is I will never learn anything from anyone at a lower stage than myself because I've already been there; I've transformed it; I've learned it. They know nothing that I don't know. At best, the relationship between a higher stage and lower stage person is benevolent, noblesse oblige. I'm going to help you to come to my stage because I believe in justice and equality, but I think it's presumptuous and I think it's wrong.

BERNSTEIN: And certainly it has been typical of many theories of development.

GILLIGAN: I would like to say, for example, that it does not explain at all why adults should be in contact with children or adolescents. It leads to a view and then an organization of human social life that is very, very destructive.

AUDIENCE MEMBER: May I make a comment with regard to some evidence about Piaget's stages? There have been some studies done where kids who reach conservation do not believe that other kids cannot also make the conserving response. Unfortunately, there is this hierarchy with certain negative connotations for those who are at lower stages.

I think that there are a variety of ways of looking at Kohlberg's stages. He looks at them in a variety of ways. There are a variety of ways of scoring them. From a strong stage theory, where Stage III presupposes, logically and empirically, Stage II, he sounds like Piaget with regard to cognitive stages. With regard to more "content-y" ways of looking at his stages, it doesn't seem that logically Stage III presupposes Stage II.

KAPLAN: I think the same can be said about say the professionals in the university. Very often it's, "Let's get together and decide on something," since we have been through the student stage we don't have to listen to them. We have to provide a show of tolerance so we get something about what they say, then we can ignore it.

FRANKLIN: What you [Carol] are saying about stage theory lending itself to this problem of hierarchization—is that specific to stage theory? Is it the concept of stage that is doing that, or does it have to do with any developmental theory that posits progress, ascendancy, movement toward some telos and the idea that this is more advanced than that?

GILLIGAN: If you had this notion of transformation, tradeoffs and so forth, then you would say as you begin to acquire abstract modes of thinking, you are in danger of losing the concrete and specific. Well, that might be a basis for a prescription that we really need children to be very closely in touch with nature or something like that to keep that vivid sense of the particular alive.

KAGAN: Before we throw out the concept, I would like to ask a question. Which domain of psychological development do any of you think comes closest to requiring the postulation of structural changes which must be sequenced?

BRUNER: Oh, wait a minute. Structural changes and stages do not necessarily mean the same thing.

KAGAN: No, I'm taking Bernie's suggestion. We can have structural transformations over ontogeny without sequencing—they're not related at all. That's the easiest form. The issue is whether one can make a persuasive case for structural changes that are connected.

GILLIGAN: Logical thought?

WAPNER: Motor development.

KAGAN: Make the case, Si.

WAPNER: Well, look at a lower form, say Coghill's amblystoma that develops a swimming response. In order to develop a swimming response there is a growth of structure. First, there is no connection from the sensory to the motor neurons; then there is a connection.

KAGAN: We know we can do it physiologically; now, let's go to the psychological domain. Carmichael put salamanders in anesthetic and found they did not have to move in order to swim and destroyed the notion that prior swimming movements were necessary. Remember, prior to Carmichael's 1927 paper, everyone was claiming that those salamander larvae had to make the small motor movements.

BRUNER: I'll be a radical again. I said you didn't need stages at all. I don't think you can possibly explain anything without talking about structural changes.

KAGAN: What about those that are sequenced and connected?

BRUNER: The thing that is interesting about structural changes is that they have this quality of discontinuity to them. If I take changes in language development, they go from the very first stage, where they're working sort of gesturally, by gaze directionals, to something like beginning to be lexical, if not grammatical. Without describing it structurally, you can't describe it.

KAGAN: Suppose I eliminated some of the earlier stages or structures. We can do that.

BRUNER: The great question is, Are there sequences of structures that are necessary and sufficient for each other? That's a more stringent question.

KAGAN: That's the question I'm asking.

FRANKLIN: I don't know whether you want to pursue this question: "If theories of development are normative and function as recommendations or as policy proposals concerning what is better or worse, then does it make any sense to talk of the truth or falsity of such theories, or of a science of human development?"

BERNSTEIN: It seems to me that the answer is yes, to the extent that we're projecting certain kinds of ideas, that we're trying to give a rational argument for this, even a persuasive one. At some crucial point, in terms of supporting it or endorsing it, you are appealing to truth claims. It seems to me that you can't give that up. You are making claims, no matter how open a critical argument is, a normative kind of argument. It isn't that I want to go back to the Aristotelian position where normative statements are true or false, but it is textured in terms of appeals to what you take to be evidence. There, you *are* making truth claims. If Carol wants to make the next move, that there is a dimension of morality which ought to be institutionalized in various ways, appealing to the kind of research that she's doing, it's perfectly legitimate to say what you have discovered about women is true or not true. And in that sense, the appeal at some point to truth claims is inevitable for any kind of argument, even a normative argument.

KAPLAN: Would you say then with respect to that truth, it is a truth that does not separate the spectator in theory from the practice?

BERNSTEIN: I'm not sure how you would interpret the term *practice,* but I would certainly want to say this.

KAPLAN: I think I'm in agreement when you say there is a truth claim. But you say that somehow we have to interpret the concept of truth in a certain way so it is not a certain kind of traditional notion pertaining to contemplated statements about what takes place.

BERNSTEIN: Well, that would get into an analysis of the concept of truth. What I think is important is that we get away from a certain interpretation of the fact-value of the Humean model and from a certain kind of ontological conception that we just read these things off from nature. I would want to say that the relationship of truth claims to a theory of development is very different than some of the traditional models, but not irrelevant.

WARTOFSKY: I asked a perverse question because I would want to argue that the truth claims of developmental theory are in no different a situation than the truth claims of physical theory.

BERNSTEIN: But that seems odd in terms of things you said this morning. If you say that in critical discourse we're projecting a kind of possibility and that we should speak about what ought to be, then, at least, we have to be sensitive to differences between that and telling whether there are quarks or black holes, and so forth.

WARTOFSKY: Well, I don't think it's a one-to-one relation, but it's a very close one because the hidden normativeness of physical theory is enormous.

BERNSTEIN: Even if there is a difference of degree, we have to recognize the difference.

WARTOFSKY: I mean, you could say for example that there *ought* to be a positron because the symmetry of the theory demands it, and so we should go looking for one. But that's not a moral law. It's a theoretical law, or, as a matter of fact, an aesthetic law within the mathematics of the theory. Then, in fact, you discover one. Suppose you had not; you have to say, well, there's something wrong here because the symmetry of the theory, which we take to be an aesthetic and heuristic desideratum of great moment in physics, seems to demand that. Yet we've looked and looked and don't find one. Maybe we have to re-orient the theory or keep looking or see what else we could do to fiddle around with this because people are unhappy about it. They're not unhappy about it in the moral sense. They're unhappy about it at the deepest levels of what counts in scientific theorizing. They'll say, "Well, but does that have to do with truth or does that have to do with taste?" I have to confess that these two values cannot be sharply separated, by which I don't mean that truth is a matter of taste.

KAGAN: No, we agree.

BRUNER: But what about the self-fulfilling fallacies that you talked about this morning? Doesn't that make it a little bit different?

WARTOFSKY: Well, I think that's a kind of devil that's staring at science all the time—looking for openings to get in. I mean, that's the risk you run because that's the way science is done. That's the paradox. It's the paradox of research. I am willing to say that it is the condition that the hard sciences are in, no less than the social sciences.

KAPLAN: Yes, I thought that was an excellent point on which to end.

FRANKLIN: Thank you all for your thoughtful and provocative contributions to this discussion.

8 Concluding Comments

Of the many issues and topics considered by the conferees, we have selected for concluding comment those that seem most pertinent to the main theme of the conference. We will first discuss the status of values as viewed from some of the main positions taken in the conference, and then we will highlight the criticisms made of values in theories of human development.

The most insistent question raised in the conference was that of the grounds, warrant, or justification for value claims. At various moments, vastly different attitudes toward values were taken, from the passionate belief that they are obligations placed upon us by a transcendent power to the conception that they are human desires conditioned by our biological natures and cultural milieus. The latter attitude takes values, espoused or enacted, as natural phenomena and, suspending any judgment of their justification, investigates them and the conditions associated with their variations and speculates about their origins. For example, Gilligan's data suggest the existence of a moral orientation different from that studied by Kohlberg and his colleagues; Kagan notes certain moral sentiments emerging at the same age in different cultural groups and speculates on their origins. Here, only empirical claims are made regarding values. So, Wartofsky and Kagan seem to agree that the role of cultural and biological forces in the parallel emergence of morals in different groups will be settled empirically. Gilligan and Kohlberg (Kohlberg, Levine, & Hewer, 1983), though their answers conflict, take the association of justice and care with gender to be an empirical question.

Other assertions made in connection with empirical questions are not themselves empirical. So, for example, Gilligan urges us to recognize and to foster that "other voice" that speaks in tones of care and interpersonal responsiveness.

159

No amount of empirical data can persuade us to agree or dissuade us from doing so. If we disagree on the values enunciated by the voice, empirical data alone cannot bring us together.

Sometimes these two kinds of assertions—about what is and about what ought to be—come close to being identified with one another when it is necessary to separate them. So, whether we are all developmental psychologists in Kaplan's sense cannot tell us whether we should be; whether the critics mentioned by Bernstein foresee a common view of a dialogical community cannot decide whether such a community is good; whether individuals embrace an ethic of care and responsiveness cannot determine whether we ought to.

In order to move from empirical claims to normative exhortations, additional conditions must be introduced. For instance, speaking about needs for dialogue and community, Bernstein concludes that "It is these fragile experiences that must be preserved and fostered if we want to keep alive the very idea of moral and social development" (this volume, p. 12). The "if" signals the critical condition but does not claim to tell us why we should keep the idea alive.

Those who study values empirically traditionally speculate about the cause of similarities and differences in values between different historical times and social groups. These speculations are attended by continuing debates about what is fixed (often equated with biologically given) and what is variable (often equated with socioculturally determined). This was clearest in Kagan's speculations about universal moral sentiments, taken to be given in our nature, and Wartofsky's countering these speculations with possible culturalist accounts.

Some might argue that the assumption that such controversies can be resolved empirically implies value relativism. If standards of truth, beauty, and goodness originate in the factual conditions of our bodies, minds, and communal lives, then are they not devoid of any universalizing power or transcendent claim on us? Do they not simply express our parochial desires and reflect the local conditions of our existence? If, on the contrary, we believe that at least *some* espoused values have a more legitimate claim on our reflective assent, then perhaps research should be directed toward better understanding the conditions under which these *values* can be made to flourish.

The interplay between faithfulness to empirical data and other norms ingredient in scientific work surfaced on a number of occasions. At one moment in the debate about biological and cultural determination of values, Bruner claimed to be bored by the fruitless contest between imperialist claims, but in other of his remarks he agreed with Wartofsky's positive appraisal of the "heuristic value" of such controversy in that each position is sharpened by the dialogue. In other words, articulating opposing conceptual approaches through controversy is valued as an end even when the debate is treated as ultimately capable of empirical resolution. Another time, Wartofsky mentioned the role of symmetry in theoretical physics as a desideratum involved in the discovery of the positron. Such norms are often designated aesthetic and sometimes included as constitutive of scientific work (cf. Solomon, 1978).

The most pointed alternative to the empirical study of values offered in the conference was the attempt to derive values from axioms, as Bruner did with his pluralistic value perspective. According to such a position particular value controversies are best reflected on by inferring and contrasting the axioms of the contesting positions. The trouble is that, being fundamental, the axioms themselves are groundless. Instead of justifying a value system by its grounds, one might attempt to judge it by its fruits, such as its "heuristic value." But what warrant would one have for the criteria by which we judge the fruits? We seem to end back where we started—with no warrant for our standards of judgment, our norms, our values.

We all proceed as though there were some sense to talking together about earlier mistakes, to learning from history, to debating what ought to be done. We do not act in accordance with the conclusion that "we have neither behind us, nor before us, in a luminous realm of values, any means of justification" (Sartre, 1956, p. 295).

Although the Conference gave few glimmerings of any exit from this arbitrariness of values, the attitude of self-examination gave rise to questions about the value presuppositions of some developmental theories. Kaplan seemed sometimes to believe that all theories necessarily assess differences and changes against standards or ideals, and other times to believe that only some theories do so and these can be distinguished from the others by calling them "developmental." In this conception, development is not necessarily ingredient in phenomena but is a function of the way we organize them. Some ways of organizing phenomena developmentally came in for criticism in accordance with apparent agreement on the idea—made explicit in Wartofsky's paper—that the norms of development are human constructions influencing the phenomena they are used to understand and, further, that we ought to oblige ourselves to reflect on, criticize, and reconstruct these ideal constructs that are both the products and determinants of culture.

Among the value assumptions brought up for critique was an assumption Wartofsky pointed to as common to many developmental theories (Vygotsky, Luria and Werner were mentioned) and embodied in Luria's work on the Uzbekhi. The assumption is that a movement from concrete to abstract is to be valued, and the state suppression of the work presupposed a higher value than this. Bruner's comments criticize the idealization of the abstract because it obliterates the context-sensitive nature of thought and demoralizes those whose traditional way of life is being devalued.

A second value criticized, especially by Gilligan, was exclusive emphasis on contract, equality and mutual respect, impersonal role-taking abilities, and so forth. She maintained that such an orientation contributes to the neglect of bonds of caring and emotional connection with one another. Gilligan also actively resisted attempts to "integrate" the two orientations she juxtaposed, suspecting that these attempts would reestablish the domination of justice over care.

A third set of values, those of technical expertise and of scientific reason, were identified in Bruner's paper as prominent in our culture and sometimes accepted without debate or question, not only in our educational systems but in psychology as well. He mentioned "cognitive science" in this regard, maintaining that exclusive emphasis on these values has been accompanied by the neglect and suppression of metonymy, fantasy, and aesthetic qualities.

Wartofsky considered Piaget to elevate, in the French tradition, logico-mathematical rationality as the supreme achievement of human cognition. Wartofsky was unwilling to accede to such imperial claims over cognition to the detriment of other modes of symbolic consciousness. These questions are reminiscent of the Frankfurt school critique of "instrumental reason" and also of other criticisms of the pretensions of scientific and technical norms to universal preeminence as the ideals of all human thought and action (Sampson, 1981).

Amidst these criticisms of particular candiates for the telos of development, at the point when the fruitfulness of the concept of stage was being debated, the discussion leader asked whether what the conferees were criticizing was any theory that posits any concept of "advance" as a fundamental principle. In this regard, the conferees had critically referred to a number of features of some conceptions of development. Kagan objected to the emphasis on continuity to the exclusion of discontinuity and categorical distinctions in common developmental conceptions, Gilligan to the notion that certain "advances" replace prior modes of functioning. It seems to us that such criticisms either cancel one another out when we try to combine them or that their proponents, despite the tone of agreement, are in conflict with one another. Replacement is a form of discontinuity, and one could not argue that a revolution in our ways of thinking about morality would be an advance at the same time one condemned replacement as derogatory toward those people whose own values are being replaced. This quandary seems to contribute to Gilligan's attempts to distinguish two distinctive moral orientations and to oppose attempts to subordinate one to the other or to integrate them. Though she recognizes two rather than many such orientations, her approach seems relativistic, sometimes implying that it is gender to which the orientations are relative.

In quite another, more frankly political, context, Bodenheimer (1971) argued that all attempts at characterizing actual changes by means of an ideal-typical account are inadequate. Whether they include stage conceptions or not, approaches assuming linear progression place highest value on stability, order and predictability, and regard social change as a process of "diffusion" from the developed to the less developed. In so doing they are blind to stratified power relations, to actual conflicts of interest, and they blink at the fact that this ideology supports the subordination of the less to the more "developed" and disguises exploitation. For the research involved to be more than an intellectual appendage to this ideology, a redefined conceptual framework is required, Bodenheimer concluded. Whether such a description fits contemporary theories of human development and whether reflection or revaluation is called for are questions remaining open for discussion.

The conferees each contributed in their own way, we think, to an enlarged vision both of value alternatives that may have failed and of new ones beckoning to us, perhaps as in a mirage, promising a better grasp of what there is and a more enduring conception of how to live.

REFERENCES

Bodenheimer, S. J. (1971). *The ideology of developmentalism: The American paradigm-surrogate for Latin American studies*. Beverly Hills: Sage.

Kohlberg, L., Levine, C., & Hewer, A. (1983). *Moral stages: A current formulation and a response to critics*. Basel, Switzerland: Karger.

Sampson, E. E. (1981). Cognitive psychology as ideology. *American Psychologist, 36,* 730–743.

Sartre, J. P. (1956). Existentialism is a humanism. In W. Kaufmann (Ed.), *Existentialism from Dostoevsky to Sartre*. New York: Meridian.

Solomon, R. C. (1978). Science, ethics, and the impersonal passions. In H. T. Engelhardt, Jr., & D. Callahan (Eds.), *Morals, science, and sociality* (pp. 311–332). Hastings-on-Hudson, NY: Hastings Center.

Author Index

Subject Index